Take a
Paddle

Finger Lakes

New York Quiet Water
for Canoes & Kayaks

by Rich & Sue Freeman

Cover Design by Lynch Graphics and Design (www.bookcoverdesign.com)

Maps by Rich Freeman
Pictures by Rich & Sue Freeman
Author photo by Andrew Olenick (www.fotowerks.com)

ISBN: 1-930480-24-5

Manufactured in the United States of America

Library of Congress Catalog Card Number: 2003097388

Every effort has been made to provide accurate and up-to-date waterway descriptions in this book. Hazards are noted where known, but conditions change constantly. Users of this book are reminded that they alone are responsible for their own safety when on any waterway and that they paddle the routes described in this book at their own risk. Void where prohibited, taxed, or otherwise regulated. Contents may settle during shipping. Use only as directed. Discontinue use if a rash develops.

The authors, publishers, and distributors of this book assume no responsibility for any injury, misadventure, fines, arrests or loss occurring from use of the information contained herein.

If you find inaccurate information or substantially different conditions (after all, things do change), please send a note detailing your findings to:
    Footprint Press, Inc., PO Box 645, Fishers, NY 14453
    or e-mail: info@footprintpress.com

Take a PADDLE

Finger Lakes

New York Quiet Water
for Canoes & Kayaks

Footprint Press Inc.

PO Box 645, Fishers, NY 14453
www.footprintpress.com

Footprint Press publishes a variety of outdoor recreation guidebooks. See a complete list and order form at the back of this book. We also publish a free, monthly ezine (electronic magazine) on outdoor recreation in central and western New York.
To sign up visit: www.footprintpress.com

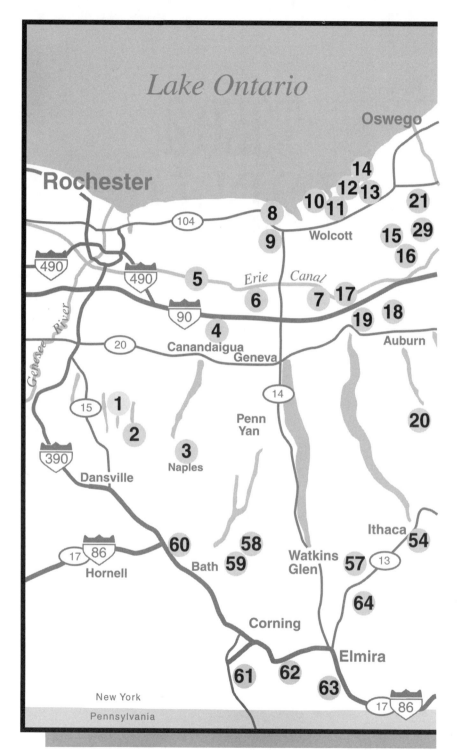

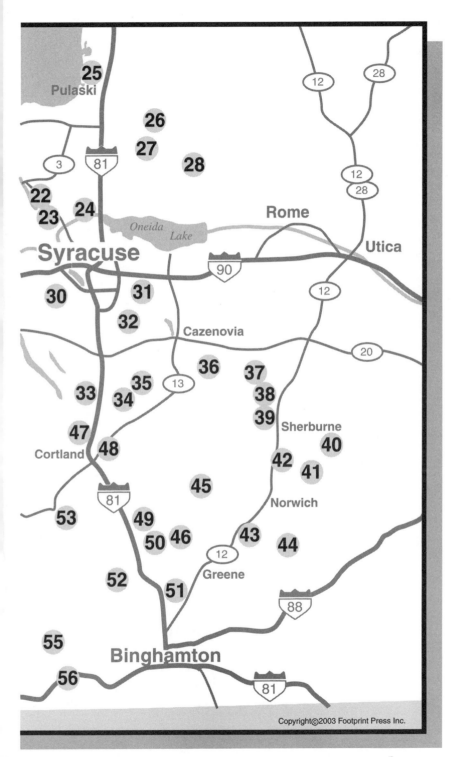

Contents

Acknowledgments

The research, writing, production, and promotion of a book such as this is never a solitary adventure. *Take A Paddle - Finger Lakes New York Quiet Water for Canoes & Kayaks* came into being because of the assistance of many wonderful people who freely shared their knowledge, experience, resources, thoughts, and time. We extend our heartfelt thanks to them all. Each in his or her own way is responsible for making the Finger Lakes region a better place to live and, most of all, a region rich with the spirit of collaboration for the betterment of all. This is what ensures quality of life.

We particularly want to thank Andy Hill who volunteered as a field editor. For our previous 8 guidebooks we personally hiked, biked and explored every trail and waterway listed. But, for this book, paddling every waterway posed a monumental task, requiring an enormous amount of time. If we paddled every waterway, the book would have been obsolete before we completed the research. To speed up the process, we enlisted the help of Andy to act a field editor. He paddled some of the waterways and reported back to us with data for this book. This allowed us to offer a more comprehensive guidebook and do it in a timely manner.

Thanks also to Susan Domina, our friend and able proofreader. Because of her attention to detail and grammatical expertise, this book is more consistent, more complete and sports fewer typographical errors. We'd like to believe it's error free but that proves to be an elusive goal that we've yet to achieve in our guidebooks.

Finally, our heartfelt thanks to Andy Olenick, a professional photographer, owner of Fotowerks, Ltd. and a personal friend of ours. He took time from his busy work schedule to capture us on film in outdoor settings. We appreciate his generosity, his professionalism and his friendship.

Introduction

Paddle sports are growing in popularity. Chances are if you've picked up this guide you're already familiar with the joys of paddling. You can paddle rapidly to get an aerobic workout or go slowly and quietly to enjoy an up-close view of wildlife afforded by few other modes of transportation.

This is not a how-to-paddle guide. Many books and instructors are available to teach you how to paddle or to fine tune your skills. See the index at the back for some local options. This guide will show you where to go and allow you to choose locations based on your skill level, time availability, and many other factors. It will probably also lead you to locations that you never knew existed as paddling options. That's a good thing. We don't have to travel around the world to find new adventures. They're often available close to home, if we only know where to look.

The waterways included are meant for beginning to intermediate paddlers or for those who enjoy the serenity of flat water. We left out white water streams, although in spring conditions some otherwise mild-mannered streams can offer white water. That's why we also recommended the best season for paddling each waterway.

Our goal is to get more people outdoors to enjoy the wonders of Central New York and to get current paddlers out more often. Have fun exploring the region by canoe or kayak.

If you enjoy this book please help spread the word by posting a review to your favorite online bookstore.

A group learning the basics of kayaking on a Pack, Paddle, Ski adventure trip.

Rights of Passage

The courts of New York State consider rivers and streams as "public highways" if they are navigable. This dates back to English common law that prevailed when our country was founded; when waterways were the major routes of travel.

Everyone has the right to paddle a navigable river or stream even if the shores are privately owned. We do not, however, have the right to picnic or camp on private property, nor to cross privately-owned property to reach the water. You can legally get out of a boat to walk the waterway or shore (to the minimum extent necessary) to scout rapids or portage around an obstacle.

Generally, the state, county or city owns the land near bridges and the roads that run next to water, so access is usually permitted in these areas. Public parks, DEC fishing access sites and state and locally owned launch sites are also available. Please obey all posted signs that you encounter.

Dogs Welcome

Many dog owners enjoy taking their companions along when exploring the outdoors - even paddling in a canoe. You must be able to control your dog to make sure an outdoor adventure is enjoyable to everyone around you, including the wildlife. Dogs are required to be leashed at a few public launches. Most waterway access points have no dog restrictions.

There are 60 waterways listed in this book that welcome dogs. Please respect the requirement that dogs be leashed where noted.

The only areas that prohibit dogs are:

#	Waterway Name
26	Kasoag Lake & Green Pond (not recommended)
29	Beaver Lake
32	Jamesville Reservoir & Butternut Creek
48	Yaman Park (take-out for East Branch Tioughnioga River)

Safety Tips & Precautions

Paddling is a sport that can be enjoyed from spring through fall by people of wildly differing abilities, ages, and expertise. To stay safe, everyone must follow simple rules of common sense and caution, which include:

- Know how to swim before setting foot in a canoe or kayak.

- Always wear a personal flotation device when in a canoe or kayak. (New York State law requires that you have access to a PFD.)

- Wear footwear to avoid sharp objects and poison ivy.

- Keep a good distance from dams - both from above and below. You could get pulled into a sluiceway, get caught in fast currents or eddys, or otherwise loose control of your boat.

- Respect the rights of property owners and obey all posted signs.

- Fast moving water can be dangerous and deadly. Use judgement in choosing to paddle a fast moving stream based on your experience and skill level. A swift current can tip your boat and pin you below water level at a strainer. You'd be amazed at how quickly it can happen. (Note the voice of personal experience here.) Never paddle during spring flood conditions.

- Cold water can be dangerous and deadly. Be especially careful if you go paddling early in the spring. It is tempting to go paddling on early warm days. Remember the water is still cold. If you do not have specialized clothing try a few of these ideas. Keep your hands warm with rubber dishwashing gloves. If you want to keep your feet warm, try knee high rubber boots instead of neoprene booties or water shoes. If you are not dressed to swim in a lake, paddle near shore so you can get to shore quickly in the event of a capsize. Paddle where wind is not as likely to be a factor, like early in the day or on smaller bodies of water. Be sure to wear your PFD as you will not be able to swim long in cold water if you swamp. Modern PFDs are comfortable and can help keep you warm. Often the air is colder on the water than on the land. Wear a hat to conserve body heat. Take extra clothes with you and put them in your boat wrapped in 2 to 3 plastic bags and seal them. Wear synthetic clothes, not cotton.

- Always take emergency supplies with you in a waterproof bag tied securely in your boat. These should include water, snacks, a flashlight, sun lotion, an emergency space blanket, a compass, a knife, water proof matches and a first aid kit.

- Let someone know where you're going and when you expect to return. At a minimum, leave a note that someone looking for you could find.

While doing research for this guidebook we paddled many miles of gorgeous ponds, creeks and rivers. We experienced wildlife up close, watched the mist dissipate from streams in early morning and thrilled to new discoveries around each bend. We also had some hair-raising experiences. The waterways where these occurred are not detailed in this book, but we do mention them so you know why we left the sections out. For instance, Tonawanda Creek from Attica to Batavia was a harrowing 5 miles of constant logjams in deep mud banks that left Rich utterly exhausted. Sue's turn at exhaustion came with a segment through Bergen Swamp on Black Creek, which was also blocked with a seemingly endless series of logjams. Instead of dealing with portages over high mud banks, Sue had to put up with knee deep nettles that sent razor sharp barbs into her legs and rampant poison ivy that left reminders long after the portaging was done.

These segments aren't in this book. Still, river and creek conditions can change rapidly with rising waters and falling trees. So a segment that we found easy and clear in 2003 can pose a problem in future years. It is impossible to predict obstructions in any given section, as one storm could change safety significantly. Paddle with caution and at your own risk.

Legend

At the beginning of each waterway listing, you will find a description with some or all of the following information:

Location: The towns and counties where the waterway is located or through which it passes.

Directions: How to find the launch point parking area from a major road or town.

DEC launch sites are often labeled with brown and yellow signs like this one for Guilford Lake.

Launch Site: More detailed information about a launch site. There may be multiple launch sites listed that give you an option of shortening your trip.

Take-out Site: More detailed information about a take-out site. There may be multiple take-out sites listed that give you an option of shortening your trip.

Best Season to Visit: The season when you're more likely to find favorable padding conditions. However, water levels are affected by many factors so there is never a definitively good time to paddle.

Nearby Campgrounds: Contact information for any campgrounds that are on or near the waterway.

Paddling Distance: The paddling distance in miles for the segment described in the paddling directions. Distance segments are also listed if there are multiple launch and/or take-out options.

15

Estimated Time to Paddle: A rough approximation of how much time it will take to paddle this route. However, time can be affected by many factors such as type of craft paddled, strength and skill of the paddlers, rate of water flow, depth of water over rocks, wind conditions, frequency of impediments encountered that require portaging, number and duration of rest breaks taken, etc.

Difficulty: A rating of the level of difficulty of the paddling experience. All waterways listed in this guide are class I water.

1 Paddle – Very Easy – A flat water pond or a wide waterway with negligible current. Suitable for beginners or a leisurely paddle by anyone.

2 Paddles – Easy – A slowly moving waterway with low probability of encountering impediments. Suitable for beginners.

3 Paddles – Moderate – A water way with moving current and manageable obstacles such as riffles and downed trees. Suitable for intermediate paddlers.

4 Paddles – Strenuous – A water way with swift current and obstacles such as riffles and downed trees. Suitable for advanced intermediate paddlers.

Water Level Information: A web site or phone number where information can be obtained on current and/or historical water levels for this waterway. Use this information to judge if the water is too shallow or conversely, too deep (flooded) or moving too fast for safe paddling.

Other Activities: A description of what you can do on or near this waterway besides paddle.

Amenities: Services and resources you'll find along this waterway.

Dogs: Tells if dogs are or are not allowed, or if they're required to be on a leash.

Admission: The entrance fee, if there is one, to use the area.

Contact: The address and phone number of the organization to contact if you would like additional information or if you have questions not answered in this book.

Maps

This book is loaded with sketch maps to give you an idea of where to find each waterway and how to navigate once you get there. We've found the *New York State Atlas & Gazetteer* by DeLorme to be a valuable asset when trying to find a launch site in unknown territory. Also, the road maps by MapWorks (www.mapworksinc.com/index.cfm) are useful.

Water access directions are listed as upstream, left or right and downstream, left or right. They are defined from the paddler's perspective as he or she is paddling downstream as per the diagram below:

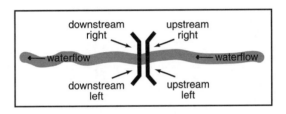

Map Legend

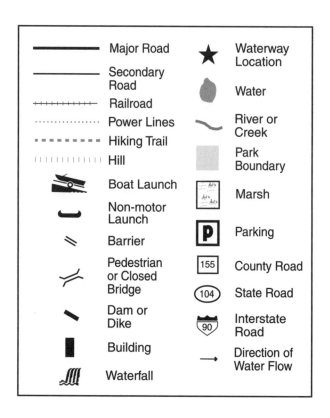

————	Major Road	★	Waterway Location
————	Secondary Road		Water
+++++++++	Railroad	~	River or Creek
··············	Power Lines		
- - - - - -	Hiking Trail		Park Boundary
I I I I I I I I I	Hill		Marsh
	Boat Launch		
	Non-motor Launch	**P**	Parking
	Barrier	155	County Road
	Pedestrian or Closed Bridge	104	State Road
	Dam or Dike	90	Interstate Road
	Building	→	Direction of Water Flow
	Waterfall		

Paddles in Ontario, Wayne, Yates, Seneca and Cayuga Counties

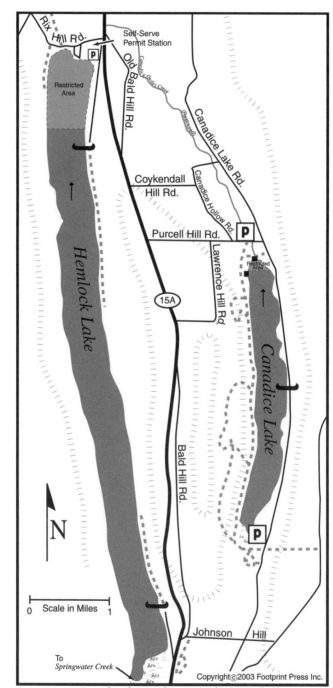

Hemlock and Canadice Lakes

1

HEMLOCK & CANADICE LAKES

Location: Livingston and Ontario Counties

Directions: From Route 15A at the north end of Hemlock Lake, turn west onto Rix Hill Road. Take the first left to find the self-serve permit station. (You need to stop here first before paddling either lake.)

Hemlock Lake Launch Site #1: From the permit station, continue south on the dirt road parallel to the lake. In 1.1 miles you come to the end of the road where there is parking and a boat launch.

Hemlock Lake Launch Site #2: From the permit station, return to Route 15A and head south. After passing Bald Hill Road (the second time) watch for a dirt road to the right. This leads 0.6 mile to the southern boat launch.

Canadice Lake Launch Site: From the permit station, return to Route 15A and head south. In 2.5 miles, turn left onto Purcell Hill Road. At the end, turn right onto Canadice Lake Road. The launch will be on the right in 1.4 miles.

Best Season to Visit: Spring, summer (water can get low in a dry summer, exposing unimpressive shorelines), fall

Paddling Distance: Hemlock Lake is 8 miles long (2,800 acres). It's 5.9 miles between launches.

Canadice Lake is 3 miles long (850 acres)

Estimated Time to Paddle: Any length of time you wish to stay out. It takes about 4 hours to circumnavigate Canadice Lake and 11 to 12 hours to circumnavigate Hemlock Lake.

Difficulty: (Even moderate winds can raise the chop. To avoid wind problems many people enjoy evening paddles on these lakes.)

Other Activities: Fish, bird watch, hike, bike

Amenities: Porta-potty near the northern Hemlock Lake launch

Dogs: OK

Admission: Free

Restrictions: Obtain a free permit before paddling (see below). Boat must be under 16 feet long and not have been in other waters for 3 days.

Contact: City of Rochester, Water and Lighting Bureau
7412 Rix Hill Road, Hemlock, NY 14466
(585) 428-3646

Long ago, Hemlock and Canadice Lakes had cottages along their shores. In 1872 the city of Rochester decided to use these lakes as a water supply. The first conduit for water was completed in 1876. By 1947 Rochester had purchased all of the shoreline property and removed the cottages in order to help protect the water supply for its growing population. Although it was very difficult for the cottage residents to leave their land, this area is now free of the commercialization that is so rampant on the other Finger Lakes.

Ninety-foot-deep Canadice Lake is the smallest of the Finger Lakes, but it has the highest elevation (1,096 feet), one of the reasons it is such a good water supply for the city. 96-foot deep Hemlock Lake sits lower at 895 feet elevation. Water from Canadice Outlet Creek is diverted into the northern end of Hemlock Lake. From there the City of Rochester Water Bureau conditions the water for drinking and uses gravity to send it north for 29 miles via large pipes at a rate of up to 48 million gallons per 24-hour period.

Early settlers tried to farm around these lakes but found the glacially scoured land ill-suited for farming. Many areas around the lakes were too steep or too wet for growing crops.

Today, the Hemlock and Canadice Lakes watershed continues to be Rochester's primary source of drinking water. The watershed covers more than 40,000 acres of land, of which Rochester owns 7,000 acres. A second-growth forest now prospers on the once forested land, and many abandoned farm fields have been reforested with conifers. Bald eagles are now present in the area (8 residents in 2003), nesting toward the southern end of Hemlock Lake.

To protect city property and the supply of drinking water, the city asks that all visitors obtain a Watershed Visitor Permit, one of the easiest permits to obtain. Just stop at the visitor's self-serve, permit station located at the north end of Hemlock Lake on Rix Hill Road off Route 15A (see the map on page 20) or download it at www.cityofrochester.gov/watershedpermit.htm. There are no fees or forms to fill out, but the permit document details the dos and don'ts to help keep the area pristine, so it's important to read it. Also, to decrease the spread of zebra mussels, it is required that your boat not have been in other waters withing three days.

Swimming and camping are not permitted. Boats up to 16 feet long (canoes and kayaks can be longer) with motors up to 10 horsepower or any level of human power are okay. The permit also has a detailed map showing the hiking/biking trails.

At the north end of Hemlock Lake is beautiful Hemlock Lake Park, which has restrooms, a pavilion with grills, and even a gazebo. Unfortunately, you can't paddle to it. Boats are not allowed north of the boat launch in Hemlock Lake or at the very northern tip of Canadice Lake.

The exceptionally well-managed watershed area contains a variety of trees, including hemlock, beech, oak, maple, hickory, basswood, and white, red and scotch pine. In addition, if you care to fish, the lakes have salmon, trout, and panfish. Or try your hand at bird watching. You may see kingfishers, herons, ospreys, as well as bald eagles near the water. The relatively undisturbed forest is ideal habitat for several woodpecker species as well as migrating songbirds.

The most scenic paddle on Hemlock Lake is at the southern end. Hemlock Lake is fed from Springwater Creek which forms a marsh of cattails, grasses and water lilies as it merges into Hemlock Lake. You can paddle up Springwater Creek quite a distance if the water is high. Both lakes are partially shielded from high winds by their surrounding hills. Try a night paddle here and let the moon and stars be your guide.

Hemlock Lake - North Launch Paddling Directions:
- Your only option from this launch is to paddle south.

Hemlock Lake - South Launch Paddling Directions:
- You can paddle 7 miles up the lake or head south to explore the marsh and creek area of Springwater Creek.
- To find Springwater Creek, paddle to the far western shore at the southern end of the lake.

Canadice Lake Paddling Directions:
- Paddle in any direction you wish, just be mindful of the wind and stay away from the northern tip.

Date visited:

Notes:

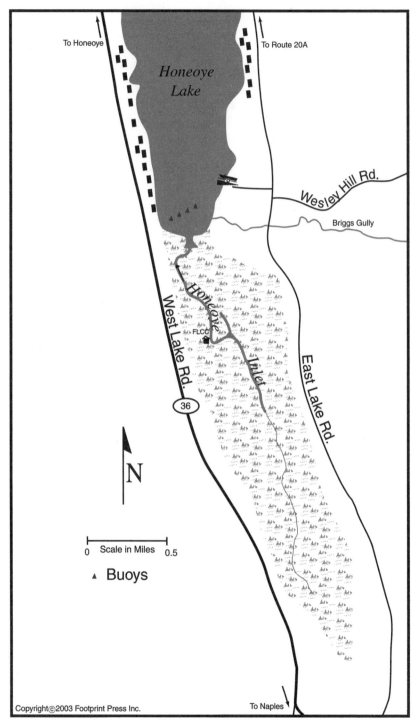

Honeoye Inlet

2

HONEOYE INLET

Location: South end of Honeoye Lake, Ontario County

Directions: From Route 20A at the north end of Honeoye Lake, head south on East Lake Road. In 4 miles watch for a brown and yellow sign "Honeoye Lake State Boat Launch" on the right. Turn right and follow the dirt road to the end.

Launch & Take-out Site: A parking area off East Lake Road, at the south end of Honeoye Lake has room for 30 cars, a cement boat ramp, a wooden dock and a gravel shore.

Best Season to Visit: Spring

Nearby Campgrounds: Tamarack Campground, 7427 Canadice Road, Springwater, NY, 14560-9704, (716) 669-2252

Paddling Distance: About 4 miles round trip

Estimated Time to Paddle: 2 hours round trip

Difficulty: ▶━━■ (negligible current, may get choked by sea weed and duckweed by late summer)

Other Activities: Fish, bird watch

Amenities: Unisex outhouse at launch parking area and a grass area with shaded benches along the shore

Dogs: OK

Admission: $6/vehicle (Mon. 6 AM - 8 PM, Tues.-Fri. 7 AM - 3 PM, Sat.-Sun. 4 AM - 7 PM, from end of April through Labor Day. Free Mon.-Fri. for persons 62 years and older.

Contact: New York State Office of Parks, Recreation and Historic Preservation, Stony Brook State Park 10820 Route 36S, Dansville, NY 14437 (585) 335-8111

DEC, Region 8
6274 East Avon-Lima Road, Avon, NY 14414
(585) 226-2466

Honeoye Lake, one of the area's Finger Lakes, is ringed with cottages. It's 5 miles long and 30 feet deep and a playground for motorboats. But, the south end is where we'll head. It sports the quiet Honeoye Inlet, a haven for beavers, turtles and more recently, river otters. In November 2000, seven otters were released here as part of the river otter restoration project. From the launch at the south end of Honeoye Lake, paddle up the winding water trail of Honeoye Inlet. If you see a river otter, fill out an otter sighting report at www.nyotter.org or call DEC at (607) 776-2165 ext. 17.

The property surrounding the inlet has changed hands recently. Owned by the Muller family since 1967, it was sold to the Nature Conservancy in 2000, then acquired by the State of New York in 2002. Today nearly 2,000 acres are managed by the Department of Environmental Conservation as part of the Honeoye Inlet Wildlife Management Area. It is one of the best examples of a silver maple and ash wetlands complex in Western New York, not a cattail marsh, as may be expected. The channel is wide like a canal, but can become covered by duckweed.

Paddling Directions:
- Head left from the launch.
- Pass buoys in the south end of Honeoye Lake. They're part of a water ski slalom course.
- Paddle upstream in the wide inlet, passing new and old style wood-duck boxes. Paddle over old beaver dams and past islands.
- Pass the Finger Lakes Community College Muller Conservation Field Station after 1.5 miles.
- When the channel ends abruptly (after approximately 2 miles) or you can proceed no farther, turn around and paddle back to the launch.

Date visited:

Notes:

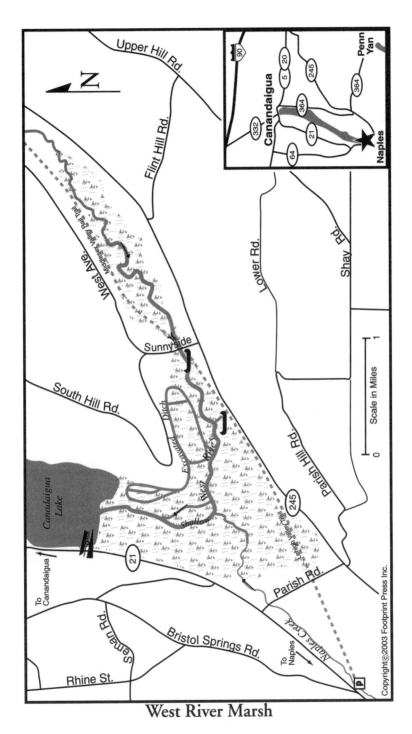

West River Marsh

3

WEST RIVER MARSH

Location: South end of Canandaigua Lake, Yates County

Directions: From Route 21 in Naples head northeast on Route 245. Turn left onto Sunnyside Road and park on the left before the bridge at the brown and yellow DEC sign "West River Fishing Access Site."

Launch & Take-out Site #1: West River Fishing Access Site on Sunnyside Road has parking for 6 cars and a sloped gravel hand launch downstream, left of the bridge.

Launch & Take-out Site #2: The launch site off Route 245 is labeled by a DEC sign "High Tor Wildlife Management Area - West River Unit." It has a two-tiered parking area and a sloped cement boat launch into a side channel.

Launch & Take-out Site #3: The DEC site off Route 21 has a large parking area, a paved boat ramp and 2 metal docks.

Best Season to Visit: Spring

Paddling Distance: About 4 miles round trip upstream from Sunnyside Road
3 miles between launches (Sunnyside Road & Route 21)
Sunnyside Road to Route 245 launch: 0.8 mile
Route 245 launch to Route 21 launch: 2.2 miles

Estimated Time to Paddle: 2.5 hours round trip upstream
2 hours between launches

Difficulty: ▶━━━ (negligible current, may get choked by duckweed by late summer)

Other Activities: Fish, bird watch

Amenities: The Route 21 launch has a Porta-potty.

Dogs: OK

Admission: Free

Contact: DEC, Region 8
6274 East Avon-Lima Road, Avon, NY 14414
(585) 226-2466

West River Marsh is part of the Hi Tor Wildlife Management Area, which covers about 6,100 acres, including high wooded hills, ravines and marshland. The cattail marsh at the south end of Canandaigua Lake drains Naples Creek and West River. In addition, ditches have been dug through the marsh to enhance wildlife habitat. This area is a major wintering and staging area for waterfowl.

West River is a lazy stream, even in spring. You can paddle in any direction you choose. One option is to put in at Sunnyside Road and paddle upstream, passing below two low bridges. This is where you'll find peace and quiet and a predominance of wildlife, including recently reintroduced otters. You may get 2 miles upstream before encountering beaver dams or a waterway choked with duckweed and have to turn around. Heading downstream from Sunnyside Road, you're likely to find an open channel, maintained by the passage of motorboats. Other channels are available for paddling, but they may be shallow.

According to Indian legend, this is the birthplace of the Seneca Indians. The Seneca tribe belonged to the Iroquois Confederacy and were known as the "keepers of the western door." The Seneca warriors where highly respected and helped make the Confederacy a strong group.

The trail shown on the map is the Middlesex Valley Rail Trail (also known as the Lehigh Valley Trail). It's an abandoned rail bed that runs through the valley for 6.8 miles from Route 21, northeast to Cayward Cross Road. You can access the trail from the Route 245 and Sunnyside Road boat launch areas. Consider combining your water outing with a hike. Or, take along a fishing pole. West River is teeming with bass, while Naples Creek is known for its trout, especially in the spring.

John Bauman enjoys easy canoeing on West River.

Paddling Directions - Upstream:

- From Sunnyside Road head upstream under the low wooden bridge.
- Paddle under the low bridge which now carries hikers and bikers on the Middlesex Valley Rail Trail.
- Continue upstream until you can't fight the duckweed any longer or until you've reached beyond your affinity for portaging around beaver dams. Then head back downstream.

Paddling Directions - Downstream:

- From Sunnyside Road head left, downstream, away from the bridge.
- Paddle around an island.
- A channel to the left goes to the Route 245 launch.
- A channel to the right leads to the excavated ditch area.
- Bear right at the next junction to stay in the main channel. (The channel marked "shallow" on the map is the original West River, but it is filling with sediment. If water levels are high, you may be able to paddle up Naples Creek for a short distance.)
- In Canandaigua Lake, bear left to find the Route 21 launch.

Date visited:

Notes:

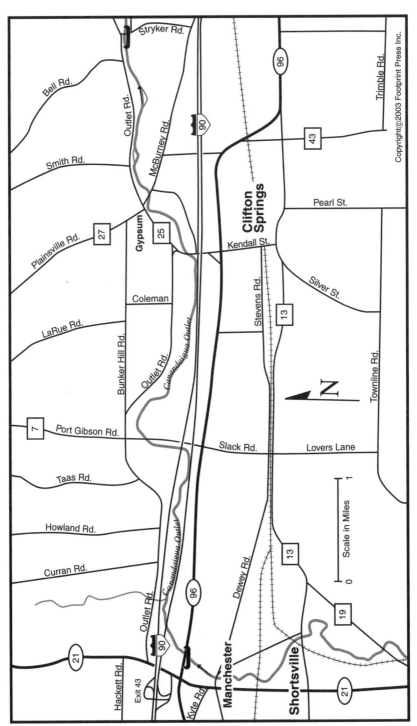

Canandaigua Outlet (start at Manchester)

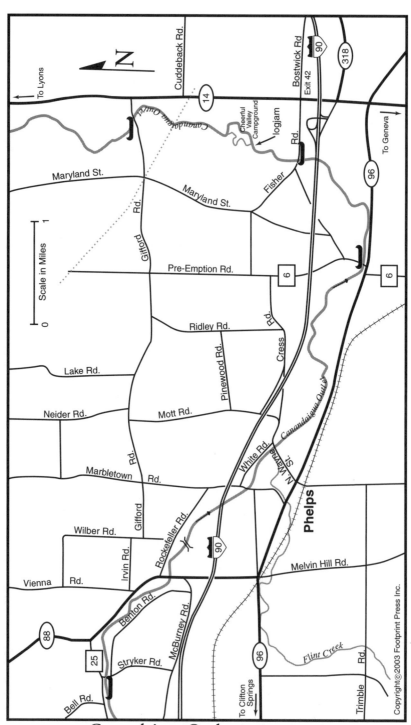

Canandaigua Outlet (end at Lyons)

4

CANANDAIGUA OUTLET
(Manchester to Lyons)

Location: Manchester, Clifton Springs, Phelps, and Lyons in Ontario and Wayne Counties

Directions: From the NYS Thruway (I-90) take exit 43 (Manchester) and head south on Route 21. Turn left onto Route 96 at the first traffic light and park at the pull-off to the right before the bridge over Canandaigua Outlet.

Launch Site #1: From the west side of the Route 96 bridge in Manchester, there's a gradual access to a stony launch point upstream, left of the bridge.

Launch Site #2: A 4-car parking area is south of the Stryker Road bridge near a sign for "Three Mills Park." A sloped dirt path leads from the end of the guardrail (don't follow the fisherman's trail behind the orange pillars) 50 feet down to water access upstream, right.

Launch Site #3 : Park at the corner of Route 96 and County Route 6 for a 50-foot carry down to water level, upstream, right.

Take-out Site #1: Park along Fisher Road, but do not block the dry hydrant. Water access is via a sloped grade, upstream, right. **Caution:** This is the last take-out before serious portages are required.

Take-out Site #2: Park along the road at the Gifford Road bridge (west of Route 14). Access is downstream, left. (It may be possible to continue paddling, but the land is posted at the Alloway Road bridge and along Bauer Road in Lyons. There is a 6-foot dam before the outlet reaches the Canal.)

Best Season to Visit: Spring and early summer

Nearby Campgrounds: Cheerful Valley Campground, 1412 Route 14, Phelps, NY 14532, (315) 781-1222
www.gocampingamerica.com/cheerfulvalley/

Paddling Distance: Route 96 to Fisher Road: 15.8 miles
Route 96 to Stryker Road: 7.9 miles (2 hrs.)
Stryker Road to County Route 6: 6.2 miles (1.5 hrs.)
County Route 6 to Fisher Road: 1.7 miles (0.5 hr.)
Fisher Road to Gifford Road: 2.4 miles
(remaining miles to dam: 11.9 miles)

Estimated Time to Paddle: 4-5 hours

Difficulty: �▬ ▬ (6-8 feet per mile gradient, moving water, debris to maneuver around)

Water Level Information: http://waterdata.usgs.gov/ny/nwis/rt (gage #04235000, is upstream from this segment of the outlet at Chapin. You can also judge water levels from the gage on Flint Creek at Phelps, #04235250)

Other Activities: Fish, bird watch

Dogs: OK

Admission: Free

Field Contributor: Andy Hill

Canandaigua Outlet runs for 38 miles from the north end of Canandaigua Lake until it merges with the Erie Canal at Lyons. As the water leaves Canandaigua Lake it follows a 2-mile-long canal with a lock that bypasses the original 3.5-mile route. From Canandaigua Lake through Chapin, Littleville, Shortsville and Manchester the outlet drops over several dams and waterfalls and tumbles as white water, especially in spring. The rest of the year the water in this initial section is often too shallow to paddle.

We're going to begin north of Manchester and paddle east through Phelps then north toward Lyons. The Canandaigua Outlet is less unruly in this section. It alternates between fast shallow sections with riffles and chutes and slow, deep sections. For the first 13 miles you'll parallel the NYS Thruway with its road noise. But you're often in remote wooded areas where birds and wildflowers proliferate. Watch for fish below in the clear water and water-swept seaweed, shaded by willows that arch over the waterway. At low water levels you may need to push or walk the stony stream bed over some shallow spots. A few old dams still exist as broken pieces along the route. They're remnants from the days of streamside mills. Past Fisher Road there are several trees and one large logjam to portage around.

Paddling Directions:
- From the Route 96 bridge in Manchester, head downstream. You may have to maneuver around debris and shallow sections.
- Pass under the eastbound lane of I-90 (a brown highway bridge) in 0.5 mile.
- At 2.5 miles pass under the westbound lane of I-90 as the outlet swings north.
- Stay left in the chute as you pass old cut-stone abutments.
- Pass under the County Road 7 (Port Gibson Road) bridge. (It is possible to park along the road and access the water here.) The outlet will begin to flow east.

- At 6 miles pass under the County Route 25 (Outlet Road) silver-railed bridge. (Land near the bridge is posted.)
- Pass under the silver-railed McBurney Road bridge in Gypsum.
- Paddle around islands.
- Pass under the Stryker Road bridge. It's a wooden bridge with silver rails. (A 4-car parking area is south of the bridge near a sign for "Three Mills Park." A sloped dirt path leads 50 feet to water access, upstream, right.)
- Run a small chute shortly below the Stryker Road bridge.
- Pass under the silver-railed Route 88 bridge. (There is a small parking area downstream, right with a narrow 50-foot path to a rocky launch at the base of the bridge.)
- Pass under an old metal railroad trestle.
- In one more mile, pass under the dual I-90 bridges.
- Pass under the silver-railed Marbletown Road bridge. (You can park off road and access the water via stones upstream, right.)
- In another mile Flint Creek merges from the right, at the North Wayne Street bridge in Phelps. (Land near the bridge is posted.)
- Next comes the silver-railed County Road 6 (Pre-Emption Road) bridge in 2.5 miles. (You can park at the corner of Route 96 and County Route 6 for a carry 50-feet down to water level, upstream, right.)
- The outlet swings north and passes one last time under green I-90 highway bridges.
- Reach the brown Fisher Road bridge. This is the last take-out before downed trees and a huge logjam that require portages. (Park along Fisher Road, but do not block the dry hydrant. Access is via an easy sloped grade upstream, right.)
- Portage around a downed tree. When you reach a football field sized logjam, follow it downstream as far as possible then portage via the right bank. It will not be an easy portage.
- Pass Cheerful Valley Campground on your right then portage around a few more downed trees.
- Pass under overhead phone lines.
- Take-out at the silver-railed Gifford Road bridge is downstream, left. (Note: It may be possible to continue paddling, but the land is posted at the Alloway Road bridge and along Bauer Road in Lyons. There is a 6-foot dam before the outlet reaches the Erie Canal. You must take-out after passing under Route 31, before the dam. Watch for a steep muddy bank to the left, 100 yards before the dam.)

Date visited:

Notes:

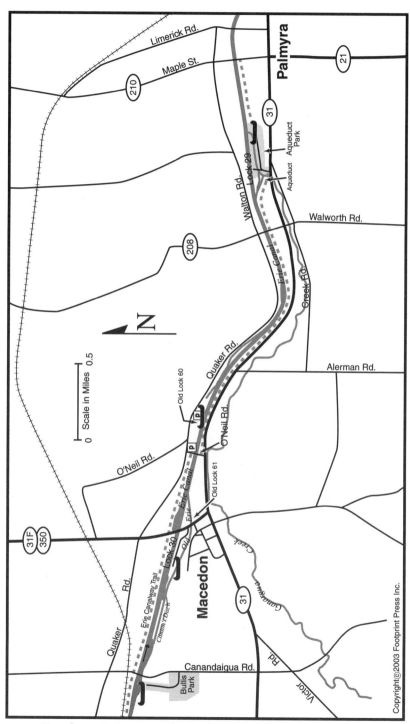

Explore Erie Canal History (Macedon to Palmyra)

5

EXPLORE ERIE CANAL HISTORY
(Macedon to Palmyra)

Location: Macedon and Palmyra, Wayne County

Directions: From Route 31 west of Macedon, turn north onto Canandaigua Road. Turn left into Bullis Park and follow the park road (which becomes a dirt road) as far back as possible. If the gates are closed you may have a 300-yard carry.

Launch Site #1: Erie Landing at Bullis Park is a dirt ramp, hand launch.

Launch Site #2: Lock 30 Canal Park: From Route 31 in Macedon turn north on Route 350. Before the current Erie Canal, turn left into Lock 30 Canal Park. Continue to the back of the park, past the Macedon Fire & Rescue building to a parking area. The launch in Lock 30 Canal Park is sloped gravel flanked by two docks that puts you into the channel of the Old Erie Canal.

Launch Site #3: Old Lock 60 Park: From Route 31 in Macedon turn north on O'Neil/Quaker Road then right (E) onto Quaker Road. Look for a small parking area on the right. It's a 50-yard carry to a floating plastic dock on the Erie Canal.

Take-out Site: From Route 31 west of Palmyra turn north into Aqueduct Park. Take the first right and follow the road to its end. There's a sloped cement hand launch and a wooden dock.

Best Season to Visit: Any time there's water in the Erie Canal (early May through November)

Locking Through: Locks operate from late May through October, daily from 7 AM - 10 PM. Nonmotorized boats can lock through for free. Bring a pair of old gloves to hold onto the cable while passing through the lock.

Nearby Campgrounds: Camping is allowed at Lock 30 Canal Park

Paddling Distance: 4.1 miles

Bullis Park to Lock 30 Canal Park launch: 1 mile
Bullis Park to Lock 30: 1.2 miles
Lock 30 to Old Lock 60: 0.9 mile
Old Lock 60 to Aqueduct Park: 2.0 miles

Estimated Time to Paddle: 2-3 hours
Difficulty: ▮━━● (negligible current of less than 1 mile/hour)

▮━━● ▮━━● (if you lock through)

Other Activities: Locking through and exploring canal history
Amenities: Bullis Park has a playground, picnic pavilions, restrooms and sports fields.
Lock 30 Canal Park has picnic tables.
Palmyra Aqueduct Park has a playground, picnic pavilions, hiking trail, historic artifacts such as the aqueduct and Aldrich Change Bridge, and a baseball field. Restrooms are at the opposite end of the park from the launch.
Dogs: OK
Admission: Free (non-motorized boats may lock through for free)
Contact: NYS Canal Corporation
200 Southern Boulevard, PO Box 189
Albany, N.Y. 12201-0189
(800) 4CANAL4, www.canal.state.ny.us

The 363-mile Erie Canal was opened with great ceremony in 1825. Dubbed variously "The Grand Canal," "Clinton's Folly," "Clinton's Ditch," and "The Big Ditch," the Erie Canal has been recognized as one of the great engineering feats of its day. With little technical knowledge or precedent to guide them, workers surveyed, blasted, and dug across New York State. They hewed through the hardest of solid rock, dug in infested marshes, devised and erected aqueducts to carry the canal across interrupting valleys and rivers, and constructed 83 locks to carry vessels through the variations in water height.

By connecting the Atlantic Ocean (via the Mohawk River) and the Great Lakes, the Erie Canal opened the West and initiated a great surge of commerce. Those were the glorious days of life at a snail's pace as horses and mules towed boats along the canal at four miles per hour taking just under six days to make the trip from Albany to Buffalo. The packet boats, dandy drivers with stovepipe hats, mule teams, and "hoggee" mule drivers are long gone. Today the Erie Canal and its towpath are used almost exclusively for recreation.

The canal was widened, deepened, and rerouted over the years to accommodate a succession of larger boats that hauled bigger loads. Initially, the canal was kept separate from creek waters by use of aqueducts and culverts. Later as engineering advanced, they learned how to control water levels in

On the Erie Canal you may share the waterway with rented packet boats.

the canal and still merge it with natural waterways such as the Seneca and Genesee Rivers. In 1917 the enhanced canal was called the Barge Canal. Today we've reverted to the historic Eric Canal name.

You can begin at Bullis Park or Lock 30 Canal Park and putter around in the current Erie Canal, the old Erie Canal and Clinton's Ditch without passing through any locks. Or, head downstream on the canal to pass through Lock 30 and Lock 29 before taking out at Palmyra Aqueduct Park. Locks 30 and 29 are working locks on the current Erie Canal. Between them is a floating dock on the canal that provides access to Lock 60, an abandoned lock from the old Erie Canal. Also in this area, but hidden from access when paddling, is old Lock 61.

Paddling Directions:
- From the Erie Landing launch in Bullis Park, head downstream (E).
- Pass under the Canandaigua Road bridge.
- Bear right at the island to enter the channel of the old Erie Canal.
- Toward the end of the island, look left to find two wood and metal posts protruding from the island. This is all that remains of a sunken barge.
- Immediately to the right, the small indent is the channel of the original Clinton's Ditch.

- Turn left to enter the current Erie Canal, continuing downstream. (Continue paddling straight in the old Erie Canal if you want to reach the Lock 30 Canal Park launch. The channel ends beyond the launch, impeded by old Lock 61 which is now a dam. Return up the old Erie Canal channel to the current Erie Canal.)
- Put your gloves on and pass through Lock 30. Hold on to the metal cables loosely within the lock as the water level lowers.
- Continue downstream. Pass under the Route 350 bridge.
- Pass under the high green arched bridge of O'Neil Road.
- Watch to the left for a floating dock. This is a good place to stop for a break and explore old Lock 60. (A Porta-potty is in the parking area on the corner of O'Neil and Quaker Roads, a 0.1-mile hike.)
- Continue downstream. You can paddle either side of a few islands.
- Pass under the Walworth Road bridge.
- Stay in the main Erie Canal channel. The old Erie Canal veers to the right, but paddling it would take you over a waterfall where the remains of the Palmyra Aqueduct are today.
- Lock through Lock 29.
- Downstream of the lock, turn right into the old Erie Canal channel to find the take-out ramp at Palmyra Aqueduct Park.

Date visited:

Notes:

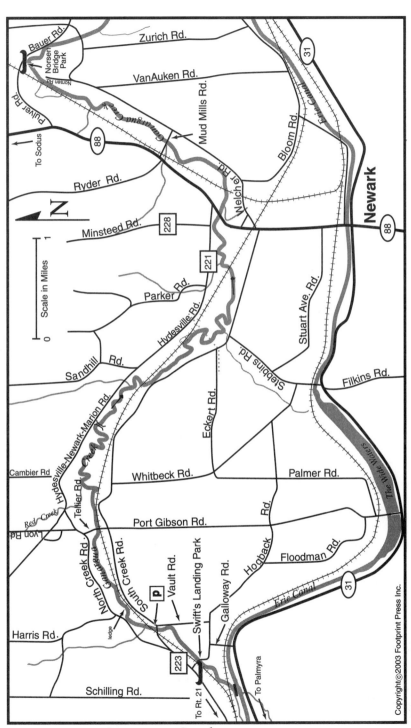

Ganargua Creek (start at Palmyra)

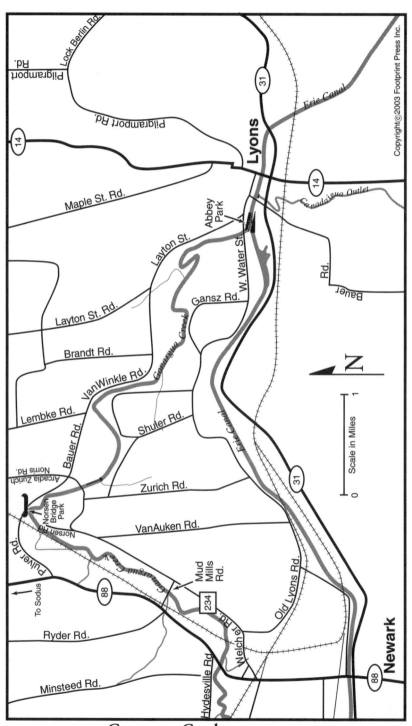

Ganargua Creek (end at Lyons)

6

GANARGUA CREEK
(Mud Creek)
(Palmyra to Lyons)

Location:	Palmyra, Newark and Lyons, Wayne County
Directions:	From Route 31, east of Palmyra, turn north onto Galloway Road. Cross over the Erie Canal and turn left at the "T" onto Hogback Road. Swift's Landing Park will be on the left before the bridge over Ganargua Creek. In the park turn left and park at the first parking area on the right.
Launch Site #1:	Swift's Landing Park, Hogback Road, Palmyra is a 17-acre park with a grass bank launch 30 feet from a large parking area. (Closed in winter, opens in April.)
Launch Site #2:	Norsen Bridge Park, 6744 Pulver Road, Newark, is a 36-acre park with a grass bank launch.
Take-out Site:	Abbey Park, West Water Street, Lyons, has plenty of parking, a boat ramp and 2 docks on the Erie Canal.

Best Season to Visit: Summer (maintains good water level all summer because it's fed from the Erie Canal) or fall

Nearby Campgrounds: Nor-win Farm & Campsite, Inc., 2921 Pilgrimport Road, Lyons, NY 14489, (315) 946-4436 http://travel.to/norwin/

Paddling Distance: Total trip: 16 miles
Swift's Landing Park to Norsen Bridge Park: 8 miles
Norsen Bridge Park to Abbey Park: 8 miles

Estimated Time to Paddle: Total trip: 5 to 7 hours

Difficulty: Swift's Landing to Norsen Bridge (Several short mini-rapids or chutes occur in the first 4 miles, especially under bridges. Be wary of potential downed trees. Colorful surveyor tape marks the preferred channels.)

Norsen Bridge Park to Abbey Park (one portage around a logjam at Arcadia-Zurich-Norris Road bridge)

Caution: The stretch from Swift's Landing Park to Norsen Bridge Park is a slalom run through cuts made in downed trees and logjams. Waterway angels have cut the passage and created a fun run. But be aware, the

passages can get plugged at any time. Without mainte-
nance this route would be impassable.

There is a dam where Ganargua Creek meets the Erie
Canal. When water is in the canal, it raises the total
water level and you can paddle over the dam and not
even know it's there. When the canal is drained, the
dam creates a dangerous drop at Abbey Park in Lyons.

Other Activities: Fish, bird watch

Amenities: Swift's Landing Park has picnic facilities, pavilions,
an outhouse, playground and a ball field.

Norsen Bridge Park has picnic facilities, a pavilion,
a playground, drinking water and a ball field.

Abbey Park has picnic facilities, drinking water,
restrooms and a playground.

Dogs: OK

Admission: Free

Contact: Wayne County Parks Department
7312 Route 31, Lyons, NY 14489
(315) 946-5836

Field Contributor: Andy Hill

Ganargua Creek's flow was tapped to provide a water source for the Erie
Canal. The headwaters are a spider's web of small brooks in the Victor,
Bloomfield and Farmington area. They merge and flow northeast to
Palmyra where Ganargua Creek flows under the Palmyra Aqueduct and
spills into the Erie Canal. This section is too shallow to paddle. The canal
waters spill over their north bank to reform Ganargua Creek east of
Palmyra. Then, fed by a multitude of small books and runs from the north,
Ganargua Creek swells to a paddler's paradise until it once again dumps
into the Erie Canal west of Lyons. Locals call this Mud Creek. Today its
muddiness or murkiness is due primarily to being mixed with canal waters.

From Swift's Landing Park in Palmyra to Norsen Bridge Park in Newark,
Ganargua Creek is a flat-water paddle with a few small chutes and white
water patches to make it interesting. It's also a slalom course around
downed trees, particularly after the 2003 ice storm. A channel has been cut
through the foliage, but the strainers would be dangerous with fast water.
It's suitable for a summer or fall paddle by intermediate paddlers who have
mastered the basics of controlling their craft. Their reward is a pleasant
paddle through fields and woods with an ever-changing array of wildlife
and an abundance of birds to observe. From Norsen Bridge Park in
Newark to Abbey Park in Lyons, the creek is wide and deep and the
current is slower, so you won't find chutes or ripples. We encountered one

downed tree requiring a portage. An east wind can add a challenge to this section.

The Town of Palmyra sponsors an annual June paddle from Swift's Landing Park to Norsen Bridge Park, which includes free shuttle service Call (315) 331-4065 for current details.

Paddling Directions:
- Head downstream from the launch at Swift's Landing Park and pass under the Hogback Road bridge.
- Shortly after the bridge an island splits the channel and creates a chute. Choose the left channel. The right is wider but is peppered with rocks.
- Pass under the brown, wooden, South Creek Road bridge followed quickly by a new-styled railroad bridge. Choose the far left channel to avoid rocks below the railroad bridge. (Parking and launching is possible between these two bridges.)
- An 8-inch ledge (old dam) spans the full width of the creek. It's easy to paddle over.
- Pass under the silver-railed Tellier Road bridge. (Water access is upstream, right via stone steps.)
- The creek will begin snaking.
- Pass under an old vine-covered metal bridge that's closed to traffic.
- Pass under a railroad bridge.
- Maneuver back and forth across the stream through passageways cut in the downed trees and logjams.
- Pass the abutments from the old Stebbins Road bridge.
- Pass under a railroad bridge (New York Central Railroad) via a chute.
- The stream widens and the current decreases.
- Paddle under power lines then the Route 88 bridge. (Access is downstream, left. Parking is possible along Route 88 and a weedy field leads down to the creek.)
- Pass under an old railroad bridge.
- Pass under the brown arched supports of Mud Mills Road bridge. Watch right just after the bridge to see the gears on the old mill. (Access is downstream left. Parking is available in pull-offs at the west side of the bridge.)
- After the railroad track comes close to the creek, watch to the left for the grass bank boat access into Norsen Bridge Park. (There is a large parking lot in Norsen Bridge Park.)
- Immediately pass the old Norsen Road cement bridge abutments.

- Reach the green metal, Arcadia-Zurich-Norris Road bridge. In June 2003 a logjam spanned the creek before the bridge and we had to portage on the right.
- The creek is now wide, deep and slow—an easy paddle through lush greenery.
- The shores will begin to be developed as you approach Lyons, a sign that you're 10 to 15 minutes from the end point.
- Pass under the wood-sided West Water Street bridge and over the submerged dam (you won't even notice that it's there).
- Bear left into the Erie Canal and head left to the launch between docks in Abbey Park.

Date visited:

Notes:

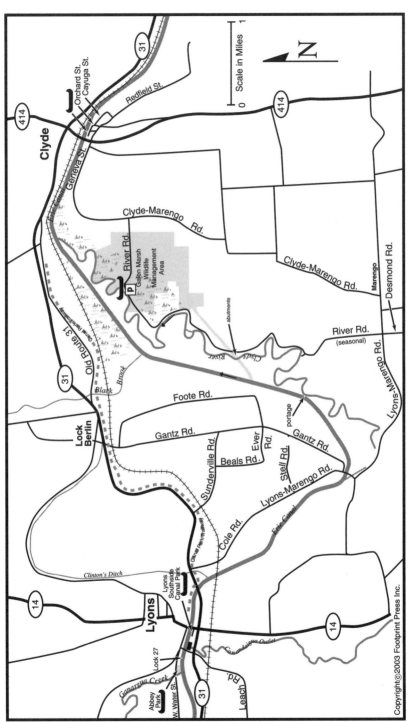

Erie Canal & Clyde River (Lyons to Clyde)

7

ERIE CANAL & CLYDE RIVER
(Lyons to Clyde)

Location: Lyons and Clyde, Wayne County

Directions: From Route 31 in Lyons head north on Route 14, over the Erie Canal, then turn left (W) onto West Water Street. Continue through Lyons until you see Abbey Park on the left.

Launch Site #1: Abbey Park, West Water Street, Lyons, has plenty of parking, a boat ramp and 2 docks on the Erie Canal. Launching here requires locking through Lock 27.

Launch Site #2: Lyons Southside Canal Park. From Route 31 in Lyons, turn north on Route 14. Before the canal, turn left into the park. A wooden dock allows access to the canal. Launching here lets you avoid going through a lock.

Launch Site #3: DEC site at Galen Marsh Wildlife Management Area, on River Road, 0.8 mile west of Clyde-Marengo Road, south of Clyde. It's a dirt parking area with access to the Clyde River bank.

Take-out Site: Canal Southside Waterfront Park in Clyde. From Clyde, head south on Route 414, cross the Erie Canal. Take the first left onto Redfield Street, then the second left onto Cayuga Street. The park is at the end of Cayuga Street with a paved ramp and floating docks.

Best Season to Visit: Late spring or early summer (when there's water in the Erie Canal)

Locking Through: Locks operate from late May through October, daily from 7 AM - 10 PM. Nonmotorized boats can lock through for free. Bring a pair of old gloves to hold on to the cable while passing through the lock.

Nearby Campgrounds: Camping is allowed in Galen Marsh Wildlife Management Area.

Paddling Distance: 14.1 miles from Lyons to Clyde, via Clyde River
21.5-mile loop starting & returning to Abbey Park, Lyons
14.7-mile loop starting at and returning to Clyde
Abbey Park to Lyons Southside Canal Park: 0.4 mile

Lyons Southside Canal Park to Clyde River portage:
3.2 miles
Clyde River portage to Galen Marsh launch: 6 miles
Galen Marsh launch to Erie Canal: 1.9 miles
Erie Canal to Clyde Canal Southside Waterfront
Park: 1.4 miles

Estimated Time to Paddle: 7 to 8 hours from Lyons to Clyde

Difficulty: (negligible current of less than 1 mile per hour but it does require one short portage)

(if you lock through)

Other Activities: Fish, bird watch, hiking in Galen Marsh

Amenities: Abbey Park has picnic facilities, drinking water, restrooms and a playground.

Lyons South Side Canal Park has a picnic pavilion. McDonald's is up a short flight of steps.

Canal Southside Waterfront Park in Clyde has picnic tables and grills.

Dogs: OK

Admission: Free (non-motorized boats may lock through for free)

Contact: NYS Canal Corporation
200 Southern Boulevard, PO Box 189
Albany, N.Y. 12201-0189
(800) 4CANAL4, www.canal.state.ny.us

This venture can be done as a linear paddle between Lyons and Clyde or as a loop. The Clyde River has virtually no current, so it can be paddled in either direction. The Erie Canal has a less than one mile per hour easterly current, so you can paddle upstream fairly easily. We did the loop from Lyons, out the Clyde River and back via the Erie Canal as a leisurely 2-day trip, camping overnight along the way. As summer progresses, the Clyde River can become clogged with vegetation. Because of the mild current, downed trees don't pose a great danger.

What once was the Clyde River has become small segments of twists and turns off the Erie Canal, leaving us a route lost in time. Even the Erie Canal in this area has a wild, forested feel to it. Galen Marsh Wildlife Management Area is 712 acres owed by the DEC. It was purchased in 1980 to preserve the Galen Marsh, known locally as Marengo Swamp.

Paddling Directions:
- From Abbey Park in Lyons, head downstream on the Erie Canal.
- Lock through Lock 27.

- Canandaigua Outlet joins the canal from the right. You can't paddle upstream because a dam blocks the outlet just upstream of the canal.
- Pass the Lyons South Side Canal Park and docks on the right then pass under the Route 14 bridge.
- Pass under the Route 31 bridge.
- Pass under the active Conrail trestle. The canal is now heading southeast.
- Bear left to remain in the canal. Clyde River heads off to the right, but the channel quickly dies out to a cattail marsh and flows through a tiny culvert.
- Pass under the Lyons-Marengo Road bridge with its high green arches. You've come 3.6 miles.
- 1.2 miles after the bridge watch to the right for a short bank. Portage over this bank to enter the Clyde River.
- Continue in the same direction you were going, but now on the Clyde River. The Clyde will make sharp bends through remote farmlands.
- At some of the sharp bends, River Road will come near the river on your right.
- Pass abutments from an abandoned railroad line.
- You'll begin to see a scattering of cottages on the right bank.
- Pass the parking and launch area for Galen Marsh Wildlife Management Area, although it will be hard to spot from water level.
- When you meet the Erie Canal, turn right to head to Clyde (or, turn left to loop back to Lyons).
- Pass under the Route 414 bridge in Clyde.
- Pass a fixed dock on the right then watch to the right for the floating docks and ramp of the take-out point at Canal Southside Waterfront Park.

Date visited:

Notes:

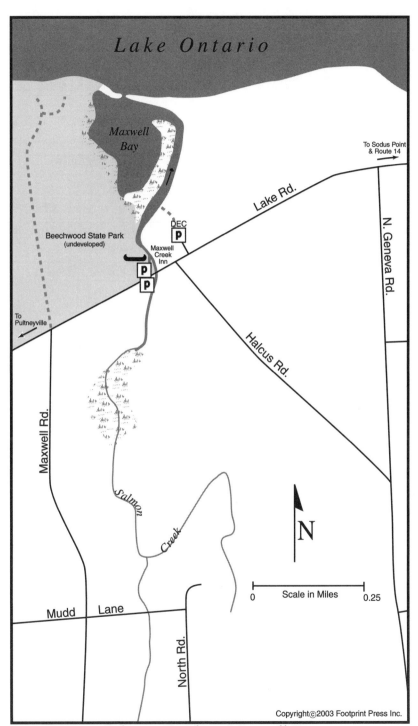

Lake Ontario

Maxwell Bay

To Sodus Point & Route 14 →

Lake Rd.

N. Geneva Rd.

Beechwood State Park
(undeveloped)

DEC
P

Maxwell
Creek
Inn

P
P

Halcus Rd.

To
Pultneyville ←

Maxwell Rd.

Salmon Creek

N

Mudd Lane

North Rd.

0   Scale in Miles   0.25

Salmon Creek to Maxwell Bay

8

SALMON CREEK to MAXWELL BAY

Location: Sodus, Wayne County

Directions: From Route 104 in Sodus, head north on Route 134. Turn right (E) onto Lake Road. Pass Maxwell Road then watch to the left for an unlabeled parking area for Beechwood State Park.

Launch & Take-out Site: From the parking area it's a 40-yard carry across grass, through a semi-circle of lean-tos to a gradual grass and dirt slope.

Best Season to Visit: Spring

Nearby B&B: Maxwell Creek Inn sits on the east shore of Salmon Creek, 7563 Lake Road, Sodus, New York 14551 (315) 483-2222, www.maxwellcreekinn-bnb.com/

Paddling Distance: Salmon Creek to Maxwell Bay is 0.5 mile Maxwell Pond is 0.2 mile long

Estimated Time to Paddle: 30 minutes to 2 hours

Difficulty: ▶━━

Other Activities: Fish for rainbow trout, steelhead and coho salmon, hike on a a network of trails (swimming is not allowed)

Amenities: Outhouses and lean-tos near the parking area

Dogs: OK on leash

Admission: Free

Contact: NYS Office of Parks, Recreation and Historic Preservation New York State Parks, Albany, NY 12238 (518) 474-0456 http://nysparks.state.ny.us/

Visiting this area brought back a flood of memories. As a child Sue spent many happy summer weeks at Girl Scout Camp Beechwood. In 1999 New York State Office of Parks, Recreation and Historic Preservation bought the camp lands and turned it into a state park. The land is undeveloped but contains buildings and a network of trails from the scouting days.

Is this Salmon Creek (one of many) or Maxwell Creek? That's a good question. Almost every written reference refers to it as Maxwell Creek, but similarly, almost every map labels it as Salmon Creek. The bay, however, is steadfastly called Maxwell Bay. Immediately north of Lake Road, Salmon Creek is snarled with a mass of downed trees so you can't paddle upstream.

Willows frame the opening from Maxwell Bay onto Lake Ontario.

But, downstream is clear and deep. The water is dotted with water lilies and is stained orange from tannin. The current is minimal, even in spring. The creek winds past DEC lands on the east shore until it bends west to meet Maxwell Bay. The bay is only about a foot deep. A high, treed bank separates Maxwell Bay from Lake Ontario, creating a great picnic spot. There is a small opening to the lake.

Paddling Directions:
- From the parking area, bear right to carry your boat through a semi-circle of lean-tos to the water's edge.
- Head downstream in Salmon Creek.
- Explore Maxwell Bay or head out to Lake Ontario.
- Return up Salmon Creek.

Date visited:

Notes:

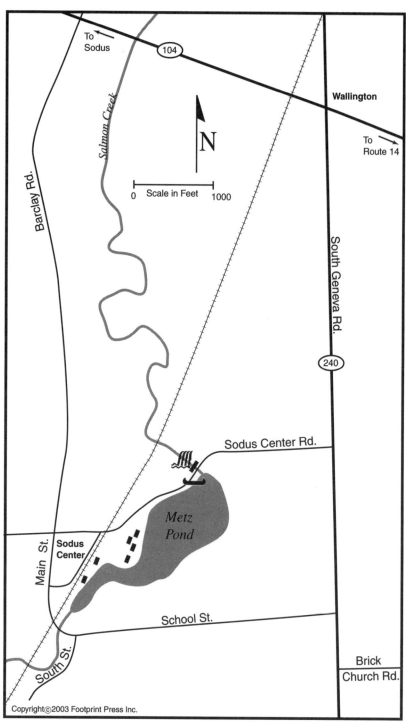

Metz Pond

9

METZ POND

Location:	Wallington, Wayne County
Directions:	From Route 104, east of Sodus, turn south onto South Geneva Road (Route 240). Then turn right onto Sodus Center Road. Cross over the Metz Pond outlet with a dam and waterfall to the right, and find the small parking area on the left.

Launch & Take-out Site: The parking area has room for 3 or 4 cars and a grass slope to the water.

Best Season to Visit: Any time; the dam maintains the water level

Paddling Distance: The pond is 0.5 mile long or 1.2 miles around

Estimated Time to Paddle: Less than an hour

Difficulty:	▬➤
Other Activities:	Fish
Amenities:	None
Dogs:	OK
Admission:	Free

Here's a small, 23.5 acre, placid pond tucked inside wooded shores for a quick paddle or to introduce a beginner to the joys of paddling. Bring kids with fishing poles and let them try their luck at catching sunfish. A few homes dot the west shore. The pond is created by a dam (with a waterfall) in the outflow on the north side of Sodus Center Road.

Paddling Directions:
- Explore at will.

Date visited:

Notes:

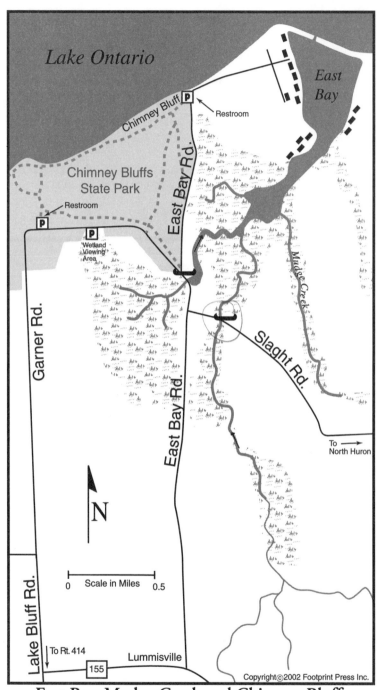

East Bay, Mudge Creek and Chimney Bluffs

10

EAST BAY, MUDGE CREEK & CHIMNEY BLUFFS

Location:	Town of Huron, Wayne County
Directions:	From Route 104 head north on Lake Bluff Road (it is the northern extension of Route 414). Continue north as it turns into Garner Road. Follow Garner Road around a sharp bend, passing Chimney Bluffs State Park. The parking area is on the right, shortly after the road becomes East Bay Road.
Launch & Take-out Site #1:	Off East Bay Road is a dirt parking area with room for 10 cars. An easy, sloped dirt launch ramp. You can't paddle under the bridge, but you can launch across East Bay Road and explore upstream from the bridge.
Launch & Take-out Site #2:	A DEC Fishing Access Site on Slaght Road, dirt parking area with room for 5 cars. An easy, sloped dirt launch ramp. You can paddle under the bridge and explore upstream from the bridge.
Best Season to Visit:	Spring, summer and fall (although the creeks draining into East Bay can become weed clogged in summer)
Paddling Distance:	East Bay Road to Lake Ontario: 1.9 miles
	Slaght Road to Lake Ontario: 2.1 miles
	East Bay to Chimney Bluffs (on Lake Ontario): 1.0 mile
Estimated Time to Paddle:	Round trip in East Bay: 2 - 3 hours
	Round trip to Chimney Bluffs: 3 - 4 hours
Difficulty:	▶━━◗ (in East Bay and its side channels)
	▶━━◗ ▶━━◗ (conditions can vary significantly in Lake Ontario)
Other Activities:	Hike trails in Chimney Bluffs State Park, swim in Lake Ontario, picnic along Lake Ontario, fish, bird watch
Amenities:	Restrooms can be found at the north end of East Bay Road and at Chimney Bluffs State Park on Garner Road.
Dogs:	OK
Admission:	Free

6/23/14 w/margs — easy launch — midway up creek ran into thick milfoil — 3 pair Heron, turtle, muskrat b.Bay beautiful — a little headwind, easy access to Lake Ontario — beautiful beach to walk, pick rocks + driftwood

Contact: Chimney Bluffs State Park
                      Office of Parks, Recreation, and Historic Preservation
                      PO Box 1055, Trumansburg, NY 14886
                      (607) 387-7041

                      DEC, Region 8
                      East Bay Marsh Unit

Four small streams drain from marshy areas into East Bay before the waters reach Lake Ontario. You can launch from two of the branches and spend a full day exploring each of the channels. The cattail-lined channels are filled with water lilies, muskrats, and a variety of birds.

If you head north on East Bay, you'll find cottages lining the banks and a few motor boats. A narrow spit of sand and rock separates East Bay from Lake Ontario. Sometimes a channel is dredged between the two. If the channel is closed, its still an easy process to haul your canoe or kayak over the land to relaunch in Lake Ontario. Only do this on a calm day or if you're experienced in handling waves crashing on shore. Bear left (W) along the shore, round a point and you'll see an awe-inspiring sight—Chimney Bluffs from water level.

Chimney Bluffs is a glacial drumlin cut to sharp spires by wind and wave action. Drumlins are long, narrow, rounded hills of sediment, formed when the glaciers scoured our countryside. These ridges sit north-south across our region and resemble an old-fashioned washboard. The drumlin at Chimney Bluffs has a high clay content. The clay acts as a cement, binding gravel and cobblestones together.

Another way to view Chimney Bluffs is by hiking the trail along the rim. Parking areas are available at the end of East Bay Road and on Garner Road. From either direction you'll climb to the top of the drumlin on a dirt trail that is often muddy and dangerously close to unstable cliff edges. This is not a place for unattended small children. Allow 1.5 hours to walk out and back on the mile-long trail. Or, head out on the trail and return along the lake shore.

Paddling Directions:
- Head downstream from either launch.
- Explore the side channels as you proceed north in East Bay.
- At Lake Ontario determine if you want to proceed into the lake or turn around.
- If you venture into Lake Ontario, turn left to Chimney Bluffs. In 1 mile you'll see the jagged bluffs towering overhead.

Tandem kayaking on East Bay

- Return to East Bay and paddle south.
- Be sure to note the channels off to the left (Mudge Creek) and right before reaching the channels with launch sites. It's easy to choose the wrong channel if you're not paying attention.

Date visited:

Notes:

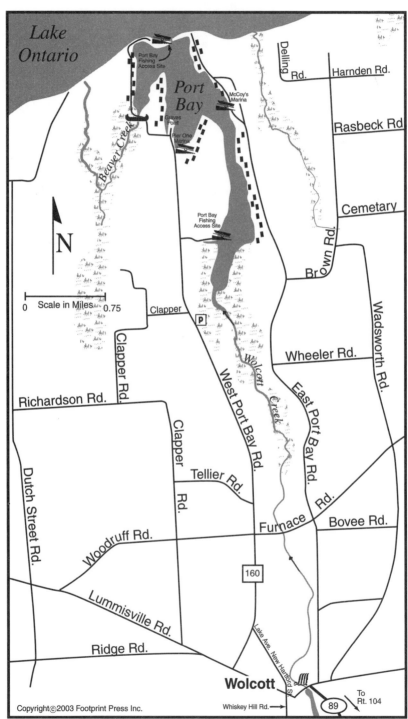

Lake Ontario

Port Bay Fishing Access Site

Port Bay

McCoy's Marina

Graves Point

Pier One Marina

Port Bay Fishing Access Site

Beaver Creek

Delling Rd.

Harnden Rd.

Rasbeck Rd.

Cemetary

Brown Rd.

Wadsworth Rd.

Wheeler Rd.

Clapper

P

Clapper Rd.

Richardson Rd.

Clapper Rd.

West Port Bay Rd.

Wolcott Creek

East Port Bay Rd.

Tellier Rd.

Dutch Street Rd.

Woodruff Rd.

Furnace Rd.

Bovee Rd.

160

Lummisville Rd.

Ridge Rd.

Lake Ave. New Hartford St.

Wolcott

Whiskey Hill Rd.

89

To Rt. 104

N

Scale in Miles
0   0.75

Copyright © 2003 Footprint Press Inc.

Wolcott Creek & Beaver Creek

11

WOLCOTT CREEK

Location: Wolcott, Cayuga County

Directions: From Route 104, head north on Whiskey Hill Road through Wolcott. The road name will change from Whiskey Hill Road to New Hartford Street then to Lake Avenue. Turn right (N) on West Port Bay Road (County Route 160). Pass Clapper Road then watch to the right for the access road to Port Bay Fishing Access Site.

Launch and Take-out Site: The DEC Port Bay Fishing Access Site on West Port Bay Road has a large parking area, a sloped cement launch and two docks.

Best Season to Visit: Spring (creek fills with seaweed and duckweed by late summer)

Nearby Campgrounds: Port Bay RV Park and Campground, 8346 East Port Bay Road, Wolcott, 14590 (315) 594-1509, www.portbaycampground.com
Port Bay Marina & Campground, 8031 East Port Bay Road, Wolcott, 14590, (888) 739-7115 www.portbaymarina.com/argo

Paddling Distance: 4.5 miles round trip

Estimated Time to Paddle: 1.5 to 2 hours round trip

Difficulty: ▶━━◀ (negligible current, wind may add a challenge, particularly on Port Bay)

Other Activities: Fish, bird watch

Amenities: Pier One Restaurant is near Graves Point. The DEC launch site has a Porta-potty.

Dogs: OK

Admission: Free

Contact: DEC, Region 8
6274 E. Avon-Lima Road, Avon, NY 14414-9519
(585) 226-2466
www.dec.state.ny.us

Port Bay is known for its abundant perch, pike and bass. It's a fisherman's haven, and therefore is popular with cottagers and motor boaters. But, head south from the DEC launch site into Wolcott Creek and you'll have serenity. Turtles and fish grow big and plentiful here. Wolcott Creek is a deep, wide channel through a lush cattail marsh. Eventually the valley through which the creek flows will narrow and present periodic wooded shores. Then the valley floor will fill with cattails and impede your southward journey. At the south end of the navigable channel we found a writhing mass of large fish during a May paddle.

Paddling Directions:

- From the DEC launch head right (S) toward the south end of Port Bay.
- Continue south, upstream in Wolcott Creek. The channel will wind but remain wide until it becomes obscured with weeds.
- Once the channel ends, retrace your path back to the boat launch.

Date visited:

Notes:

12

BEAVER CREEK

Location: Wolcott, Cayuga County (see map on page 60)

Directions: From Route 104, head north on Whiskey Hill Road through Wolcott. The road name will change from Whiskey Hill Road to New Hartford Street then to Lake Avenue. Turn right (N) on West Port Bay Road (County Route 160). Pass the first Port Bay Fishing Access Site, then bear left away from Graves Point. Park at the pull-out area labeled "Anglers Park Here" on the left, shortly before Beaver Creek.

Launch and Take-out Site #1: From the angler's parking area it's a short carry to the bank of Beaver Creek.

Launch and Take-out Site #2: Continue to the end of West Port Bay Road at Lake Ontario. To the right is "Port Bay Fishing Access Site," a narrow road across the gravel bank to a sloped cement launch and dock into Port Bay.

Best Season to Visit: Spring

Nearby Campgrounds: (See Wolcott Creek on page 61.)

Paddling Distance: 4 miles round trip in Beaver Creek

The Port Bay, Beaver Creek, Lake Ontario loop is 4.2 miles long

Estimated Time to Paddle: 2 hours to explore Beaver Creek

2 to 3 hours to circumnavigate from the DEC launch down Port Bay to explore Beaver Creek then return to the launch via Lake Ontario.

Difficulty: ▬▬ (negligible current, wind can be a challenge on Port Bay)

▬▬ ▬▬ (conditions can vary significantly on Lake Ontario)

Other Activities: Fish, bird watch

Amenities: Porta-potty at the Port Bay Fishing Access Site

Dogs: OK

Admission: Free

Contact: DEC, Region 8
6274 E. Avon-Lima Road, Avon, NY 14414-9519
(585) 226-2466
www.dec.state.ny.us

You have a choice here. The first option is to launch into Beaver Creek and paddle through a landscape of cattail marsh and scrub brush, away from busy Port Bay. Or, embrace the diversity and launch from the northern Port Bay Fishing Access Site. Paddle past cottages on Port Bay, then explore Beaver Creek, including the northern branch that leads to Lake Ontario. Here, drag across the treed gravel bar (snack break, anyone?) and return to the launch point via Lake Ontario. Of course, before embarking on this circular route, check the water conditions on Lake Ontario. We paddled it on a glass-smooth May day, but the lake can get very rough.

Beaver Creek is a very easy paddle. The vegetation closes in on you a few times, but you can easily push through branches and the channel will quickly open up again. The bends keep you guessing what's around the next corner. It could be water lilies, beaver dens, or other surprises.

Beaver Creek Paddling Directions:
- From the West Port Bay Road bank, head downstream.
- Pass the channel to the right and continue straight until you can go no further, a total of approximately 1 mile.
- On the way back, bear left to explore the northern channel which is 1.2 miles long. This will lead to a gravel bank along Lake Ontario—a fine spot for a picnic.
- Return down this channel and turn left to follow the main Beaver Creek channel back to West Port Bay Road.

Loop Paddling Directions:
- From the DEC launch at the end of West Port Bay Road, launch into Port Bay.
- Bear right and paddle south across Port Bay for 0.8 mile, passing cottages.
- If you're not claustrophobic, you may be able to paddle through the big culvert under West Port Bay Road to enter Beaver Creek. Otherwise, it's a quick, easy portage across the road.
- Explore as much of Beaver Creek as you want, then eventually take the northern channel toward Lake Ontario.
- Portage over the treed gravel bank along Lake Ontario and paddle to the right, along the shore for 1.2 miles.
- Paddle around a big metal breakwall into the Port Bay channel.
- Bear right in Port Bay to return to the launch.

Date visited:

Notes:

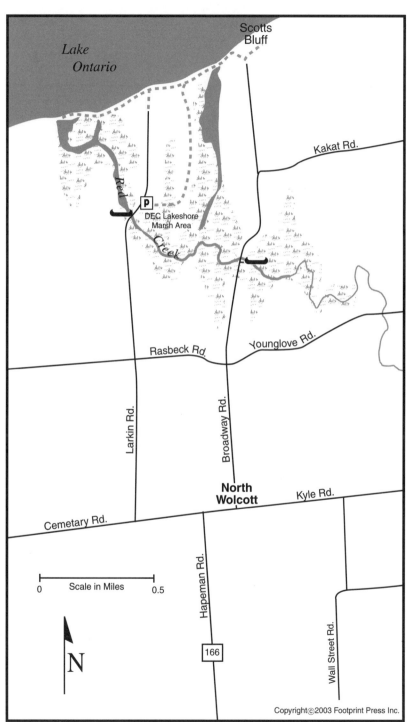

Red Creek Marsh

13

RED CREEK MARSH

Location: North Wolcott, Wayne County

Directions: From Route 104, turn north onto Whiskey Hill Road into Wolcott. At the Venus statue, turn right onto Main Street, then take the next left onto Mill Street. Pass Wolcott Falls, then turn left onto East Port Bay Road. Turn right (E) onto Furnace Road. After 1.5 miles, turn left (N) on Hapeman Road. Jog right onto Cemetery Road, then a quick left onto Broadway Road. Pass Younglove Road, then watch on the right for Lakeshore Marsh Area parking.

Launch & Take-out Site: The Lakeshore Marsh Area parking lot off Broadway Road holds 12 cars. You can launch from the creek bank near the parking lot or there's a sloped launch upstream, left of the bridge.

Best Season to Visit: Spring and summer (avoid fall hunting season)

Nearby Campgrounds: Cherry Grove Campground & Charters, 12669 Ridge Road, Wolcott, NY 14590, (315) 594-8320 www.lakeontario.net\cherrygrove\

Paddling Distance: 2.8 miles round trip
Broadway Road to Larkin Road is 0.7 mile
Larkin Road to Lake Ontario is 0.7 mile

Estimated Time to Paddle: 1 hour

Difficulty: ▶━━━ (negligible current unless the openings to Lake Ontario have been breached; possible wind off Lake Ontario)

Other Activities: Hike to Scotts Bluff, walk or picnic along the beach, bird watch

Amenities: None

Dogs: OK

Admission: Free

Contact: DEC, Region 8
6274 E. Avon-Lima Road, Avon, NY 14414-9519
(585) 226-2466

Red Creek is a naturally impounded waterway, blocked from Lake Ontario by a gravel bank that can become a several feet high pile of rocks when storms sweep across Lake Ontario. It's part of the Lake Shore Marshes Wildlife Management Area, managed by DEC. Paddle wide, deep channels through cattails and water lilies to the gravel bank. Then, if you want, walk the beach and climb to the 100-foot-high Scotts Bluff. The bluff is a wind and water sculpted drumlin left by the glaciers.

Paddling Directions:
- Head downstream under the Broadway Road bridge from the launch area.
- Paddle under a low rusted metal bridge at Larkin Road.
- Pull your boat up on the gravel bank at Lake Ontario if you want to hike to the top of Scotts Bluff. Otherwise, simply retrace your path back to the launch.

Date visited:

Notes:

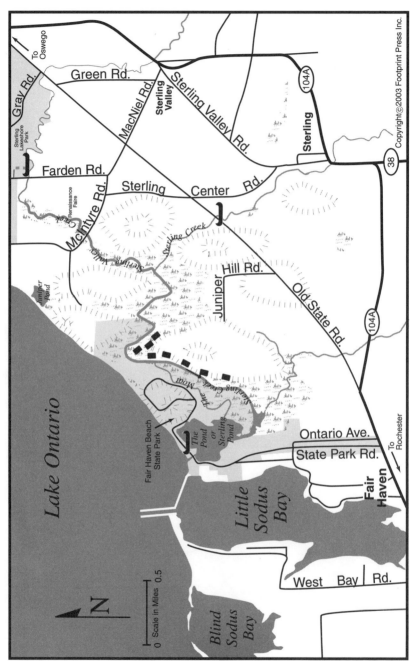

Sterling Valley Creek & Sterling Creek

14

STERLING VALLEY CREEK
& STERLING CREEK

Location: North Sterling to Fair Haven, Cayuga County

Directions: Sterling Lakeshore Park is off Route 104A, between Fair Haven and Oswego. From Route 104A in Sterling Valley, head west on MacNiel Road, then north on Farden Road. Cross Sterling Valley Creek, then turn right into a dirt and grass 2-track between wooden posts. It leads to a small parking area.

Launch Site #1: Sterling Lakeshore Park hand launch site off Farden Road is at the end of a dirt and grass 2-track with a couple parking spaces at the end. A yellow sign points right to Trail #11 and left to the boat launch. It's a 50-yard carry along the trail to wooden steps and a dock. Watch for poison ivy.

Launch Site #2: You can park along Old State Road. A sloped launch is upstream, left of the bridge over Sterling Creek.

Take-out Site: The boat launch at Fair Haven Beach State Park. Inside Fair Haven Beach State Park continue around Sterling Pond, over the pond outlet to the first parking lot on the right. There's a sloped launch and gradual sand banks, both great for launching or take-out. _– yes_

Best Season to Visit: Spring to early summer (can be choked with duckweed by late summer) _was great 9/17/19,_

Nearby Campgrounds: Fair Haven Beach State Park, Route 104A, PO Box 16, Fair Haven, NY 13064, (315) 947-5205

Paddling Distance: Total Distance: 5.6 miles
Farden Road to McIntyre Road: 1.2 miles
McIntyre Road to Fair Haven State Park: 4.4 miles

Estimated Time to Paddle: 2 hours

Difficulty: ▬▬◖ (negligible current, even in spring, wind may add a challenge)

Other Activities: Fish, bird watch, hike, picnic, swim, attend the Renaissance Festival

Amenities: Sterling Lakeshore Park has hiking trails, a nature center, restrooms
Fair Haven Beach State Park has camping, hiking trails, swimming, picnic facilities, boat rental, restrooms

Dogs:	OK
Admission:	Free launch at Sterling Lakeshore Park and off Old State Road
	$6/vehicle admission to Fair Haven Beach State Park
Contact:	Sterling Nature Center
	PO Box 216, Sterling, NY 13156
	(315) 947-6143, www.cayuganet.org/sterlingpark/

Fair Haven Beach State Park
Route 104A, PO Box 16, Fair Haven, NY 13064
(315) 947-5205, http://nysparks.state.ny.us/parks/

Coming through the tunnel under Farden Road on Sterling Valley Creek.

There are at least four choices for paddling this area. We describe starting at Sterling Lakeshore Park and paddling downstream to Sterling Pond in Fair Haven Beach State Park. If it's a windy day, you may find reversing this direction to be an easier paddle. The third option is to put in at the Fair Haven Beach State Park launch and paddle Sterling Pond and Sterling Creek for a ways then returning to your launch point. Finally, to avoid paying for entrance to Fair Haven Beach State Park, you could paddle between the launches on Farden Road and Old State Road, a distance of 2.8 miles one-way.

Sterling Lakeshore Park is a spectacular 1,400-acre site, with nearly two miles of Lake Ontario shoreline, a nature center and plenty of hiking trails. It features glacially sculpted bluffs with scenic vistas of Lake Ontario.

Sterling Valley Creek winds through a wildlife-rich cattail marsh before merging with Sterling Creek. Both creeks are wide and gentle. Take your binoculars to enjoy the many hawks, herons, ducks, geese, turtles, and frogs you'll find along the way.

A beaver den along Sterling Creek.

Paddling Directions:
- From the launch at Farden Road head downstream under the bridge.
- At McIntyre Road (after 1.2 miles) duck through the culvert. (It's an easy portage to the left if the water level is high.)
- Continue straight as Sterling Creek merges from the left. (You can paddle up Sterling Creek to the launch at Old State Road and farther until it becomes impassible near Route 104A.)
- Bear left to stay in the creek. (To the right is a smaller channel for The Moat—an impenetrable swamp filled with downed trees and teeming with wildlife. Explore some of the cuts into The Moat if you wish to enjoy the turtles, ducks and aquatic plants.)
- Stay in the wide channel until you reach Sterling Pond.
- Cross the pond toward Lake Ontario to the point of land east of the channel to Lake Ontario. 481N to 104A (thruOswego)

Date visited: 9/17/19 - Put in @ Fair Haven State Park. Great parking, access. Cross Sterling Pond

Notes: 6/19 + head to river. Herons, beaver dam. Did not make it up to Rennaussance, ran out of time. No place to pull off + pee, otherwise, great paddle.

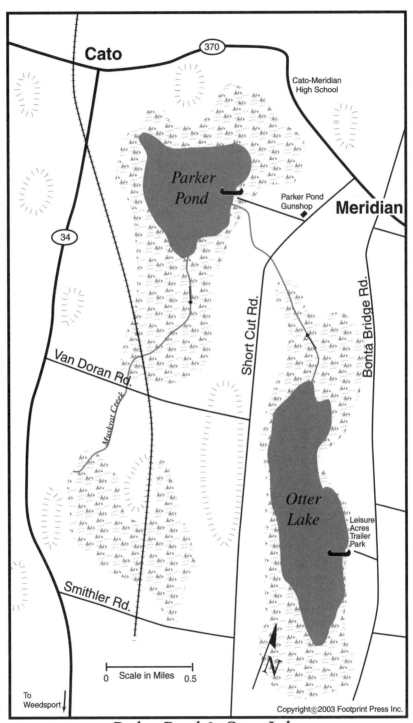

Parker Pond & Otter Lake

15

PARKER POND

Location:	Cato, Cayuga County
Directions:	Exit I-90 at Weedsport (exit 40) and head north on Route 34. Turn right (E) on Van Doran Road, then left (N) on Short Cut Road. Cross over the channel that connects Otter Lake and Parker Pond, then watch for the Parker Pond Gun Shop on the left.

Launch & Take-out Site : At the Parker Pond Gun Shop boat launch, a dirt ramp.

Best Season to Visit: Spring and summer (avoid fall hunting season)

Nearby Campgrounds: Cross Lake Park Campground, 12946 Dugar Road, Cato, NY 13033, (315) 678-2143

Paddling Distance: 2.3 miles around the lake

Estimated Time to Paddle: 1-2 hours

Difficulty: ►━━●

Other Activities: Fish, bird watch

Amenities: None

Dogs: OK

Admission: $5 per boat

Contact: Parker Pond Gun Shop
11259 Short Cut Road, Cato, NY 13080
(315) 626-2605

Parker Pond or Parker's Pond, take your choice. By either name, it's small —only 0.3 square miles. And, it's shallow—only 6 to 7 feet deep. But it's also pristine. This pond has an organic bottom and is a flood zone, so there can be no development along the shores. Aren't we lucky? Try a paddle here in spring when the ducks and geese are migrating.

Paddling Directions:
• Explore at will.

Date visited:

Notes:

16

OTTER LAKE

Location: Cato, Cayuga County (see map on page 72)
Directions: Exit I-90 at Weedsport (exit 40) and head north on
                      Route 34. Turn right (E) on Jorolemon Road then left
                      (N) on Bonta Bridge Road. Pass Lockwood Road then
                      turn left into Leisure Acres Trailer Park at the sign. The
                      launch is at the end of the road.
Launch & Take-out Site : At the Leisure Acres Trailer Park boat launch.
Best Season to Visit: Spring, summer and fall
Nearby Campgrounds: Cross Lake Park Campground, 12946 Dugar Road,
                      Cato, NY 13033, (315) 678-2143
Paddling Distance: 3.4 miles around the lake
Estimated Time to Paddle: 2 hours
Difficulty: ▶━━━◣
Other Activities: Fish, bird watch
Amenities: None
Dogs: OK
Admission: $5 per boat, open May through September
Contact: Leisure Acres Trailer Park
                      10857 Bonta Bridge Road, Cato, NY 13080
                      (315) 626-6560

Small can be a good thing. Otter Lake covers 0.43 square miles and is only 8 feet deep, but that's plenty of water for a quiet paddle among an abundance of wildlife. The shores are wooded wetlands. Water from Otter Lake drains through the wetlands to the even smaller Parker Pond.

Paddling Directions:
  • Explore at will.

Date visited:

Notes:

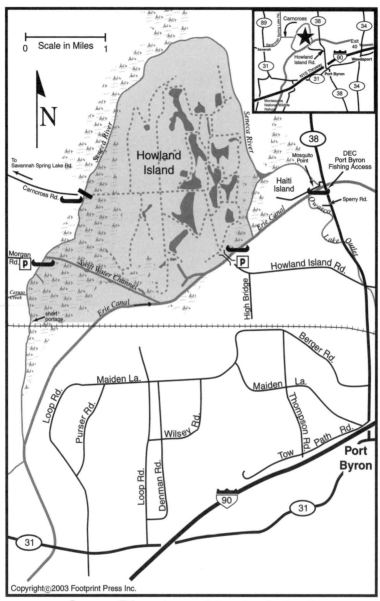

Seneca River (around Howland Island)

17

SENECA RIVER
(around Howland Island)

Location:	Savannah, Wayne & Cayuga Counties
Directions:	From Port Byron, head north on Route 38 for 3 miles. Just before the bridge over the Erie Canal/Seneca River, a DEC launch labeled "Port Byron Fishing Access Site" is on the left.
Launch Site #1:	The Port Byron Fishing Access Site has a gravel boat ramp and parking for 10 cars.
Launch Site #2:	From the end of Howland Island Road, carry your boat 20 yards downhill to the right to put in downstream of the bridge. (The old launch site is across Howland Island bridge on the opposite bank of the Erie Canal.) Parking on the right side of Howland Island Road, before the bridge is very limited. The bridge is closed to traffic.
Launch Site #3:	From Savannah Spring Lake Road, turn east onto Morgan Road. Park at the DEC office at the end of the road and carry your boat 400 yards via an old dirt road to water's edge.
Launch Site #4:	A parking area at the end of Carncross Road provides easy access to the gravel dike across the Seneca River. There is no ramp, but the dike makes an easy launch site.
Take-out Site:	Since this is a circular route you can launch and take-out at any of the three spots. Or, launch from one spot and leave a car at another for take-out.

Clogged w/lilypads in Sept [handwritten note pointing to Launch Site #1]

Best Season to Visit: Spring or summer (avoid fall hunting season)

Paddling Distance: Total loop : 10.7 miles

Route 38 northwest to Carncross Road: 5.6 miles

Carncross Road to Howland Island Road (via Swift Water Channel): 3.7 miles

Howland Island Road to Route 38: 1.4 miles

(The loop around Haiti Island is 2.7 miles long.)

Estimated Time to Paddle: 3 to 4 hours

Difficulty:

Other Activities: Fish, bird watch, hike or bike on Howland Island
Amenities: None
Dogs: OK
Admission: Free
Contact: NYS Canal Corporation
200 Southern Boulevard, PO Box 189, Albany 12201
(800) 4CANAL4, www.canal.state.ny.us

DEC, Region 8
1385 Morgan Road, Savannah, NY 13146
(315) 365-2134, www.dec.state.ny.us

An easy paddle around Howland Island.

Howland Island is part of the Northern Montezuma Wildlife Management Area and is managed by DEC. It was formed in the early 1900s with the building of the Barge Canal. In some portions the Barge Canal uses the Seneca River basin, but here the canal channel was cut across the southern section of a big loop in the river. The island is accessed only by pedestrian bridges. It is maintained for waterfowl nesting habitat and is networked with trails for hiking and bicycling. You can land anywhere on the island for a break or picnic.

Most of the water flow is now routed through the Erie Canal (the Barge Canal has reverted to its historical name), leaving minimal flow in the Seneca River. It also tends to fill with silt, which can make paddling tedious in low water conditions. In May we found deep water for the entire route. If the wind is blowing from its usual westerly direction, paddling counterclockwise will be easier through the western sections.

Cottages dot the shore of Haiti Island. They become sparse and eventually disappear as you head north along Howland Island. Soon, your only company will be the numerous great blue herons, an eagle if you're lucky, and the many patches of water lilies. The channel is wide and deep, so downed trees from the 2003 ice storm don't impede your progress except in one spot where you need to duck under a downed tree. Round the bend to head south and the forest gives way to a grassland marsh. Contrary to it's name, Swift Water Channel is not swift, it's only straight and rather boring. You may encounter motorboats on the Erie Canal, but fortunately that's a short segment of this route.

Paddling Directions
(from the Port Byron, Route 38 Fishing Access Site):
- From the the Port Byron Fishing Access Site near Mosquito Point, head across the Erie Canal and under the smaller, wood-planked Haiti Island bridge into the Seneca River.
- Turn right to continue in the Seneca River and leave Haiti Island behind. (If you bear left it's 2.7 miles around Haiti Island.)
- The Seneca River will bend left and eventually head south. You'll leave forest behind and enter marshlands.
- At the Carncross Road entrance to Howland Island, you'll have to portage over the small earthen dam. You've paddled 5.6 miles. (This is an access site.)
- Turn left into the Swift Water Channel.
- Turn left to enter the Erie Canal.
- Pass under the closed Howland Island Road bridge. (The official launch area is downstream, left. Downstream, right has the shortest access to parking.)
- Pass the Haiti Island channel (marker R500) to the left. Stay in the Erie Canal.
- Owasco Outlet merges from the right.
- Bear right for the take-out point before the Route 38 bridge.

Date visited:

Notes:

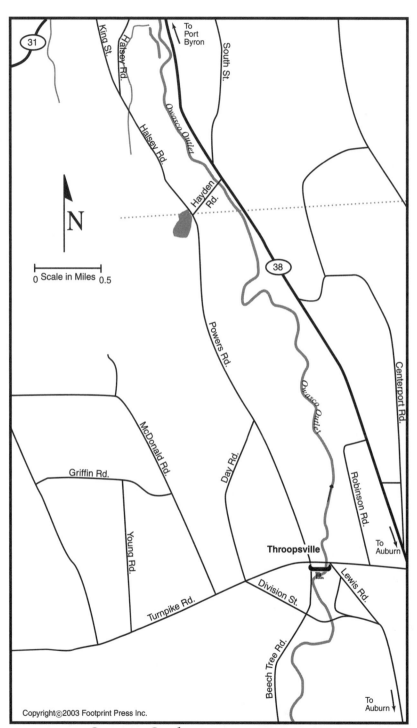

Owasco Outlet (start at Throopsville)

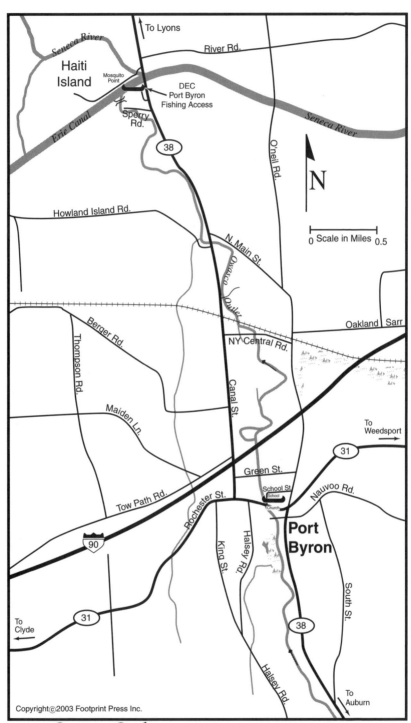

Owasco Outlet (end at Seneca River/Erie Canal)

18

〜⁓

OWASCO OUTLET
(Throopsville to Seneca River/Erie Canal)

Location: North of Auburn, Cayuga County

Directions: From Auburn take Route 38 north, then turn left (W) on Turnpike Road for 0.6 mile to Throopsville. There is a small pull-off area on the right just after the bridge in Throopsville.

Launch Site #1: Launch from the southwest (upstream) side of the Turnpike Road bridge in Throopsville. A steep bank will lead down to a gravel bar where you can launch between the waterfall and the bridge. (Notice remains of an old mill parallel to the road.)

Launch Site #2: In Port Byron (Rochester Street, Route 31) park at the bend in School Street near the school and cross a mowed grass field to a sloped bank near the first tree below the Route 31 bridge. Or, park at the St. John's Church parking lot.

Take-out Site: From Port Byron, head north on Route 38. The DEC "Port Byron Fishing Access Site" is on the left just before the bridge over the Seneca River/Erie Canal. There's parking for 15 cars and a sloped gravel launch.

Best Season to Visit: Late spring (for the full route, but avoid it when the water is very fast)

Spring, summer and fall (Port Byron to Seneca River)

Paddling Distance: Total: 9.6 miles

Throopsville to Port Byron: 4.1 miles

Port Byron to Seneca River: 5.5 miles

Estimated Time to Paddle: 3 hours

Difficulty: ►━◗ ►━◗ (fast-moving stream with riffles and shallow spots plus a few downed trees to portage around)

Other Activities: None

Amenities: In Port Byron a few restaurants are to the west of the outlet.

At the take-out, on the north side of the Route 38 bridge over the Seneca River is Pirates Landing Restaurant.

Dogs:	OK
Admission:	Free

The Owasco Outlet runs from the north end of Owasco Lake through Auburn. It then continues north through Throopsville and Port Byron and eventually meets the Seneca River near Haiti Island at an area called Mosquito Point. The Seneca River is also part of the Erie Canal in this section. (See page 76 for a description of the route around Howland Island from here.)

Since a dam impedes Owasco Outlet in Auburn and is followed by 4 miles of falls, dams, logjams and gorges, we'll start farther downstream in Throopsville. From Throopsville north to the Seneca River expect a moving current of crystal clear water through a rocky creekbed. Fish watching in the clear water was a favored pastime of ours as we paddled. Of course, the clear water also gives you prime view of the tires that litter the creekbed downstream from Port Byron.

In early spring or after heavy rains the current can get particularly brisk and some of the riffles might qualify as white water. So, pick a calmer time to paddle. From Throopsville to Port Byron the channel wanders between steep wooded cliffs making this a gorgeous route to paddle. There are picnic spots available at the school grounds in Port Byron and flat gravel banks along the shore north of Port Byron.

Paddling Directions:
- Head downstream from the Turnpike Road bridge in Throopsville.
- There will be a section of riffles (or white water depending on the speed of the current).
- Pass under the cement and guardrail bridge of Hayden Road.
- Pass under a small rusted metal bridge and some riffles as you approach Port Byron.
- At about the 5 mile point, see a church on your right. Look carefully at the bank on the right to see a culvert dating back to the first Erie Canal (Clinton's Ditch). Then pass under the cement and silver-railed Route 31 bridge in Port Byron. (Take-out is downstream, right near the first tree. A short bank leads to a grassy school yard which would make a nice picnic area.)
- Pass the old Green Street bridge abutments. (A new bridge may be in place when you paddle here.)
- Pass under the high I-90 bridges at about 5.5 miles.
- Pass under the NY Central Road bridge with rusted white guardrails.
- Pass under the Conrail railroad bridge.
- Pass under a private one-lane bridge.

- Pass under the green metal Canal Street (Route 38) bridge.
- Portage around downed trees.
- Pass abutments that used to support a Sperry Road bridge and a swinging pedestrian bridge as you approach the Seneca River/Erie Canal.
- Turn right into the Seneca River/Erie Canal (downstream) and look for the take-out point on the right before the Route 38, arched green superstructure bridge.

Date visited:

Notes:

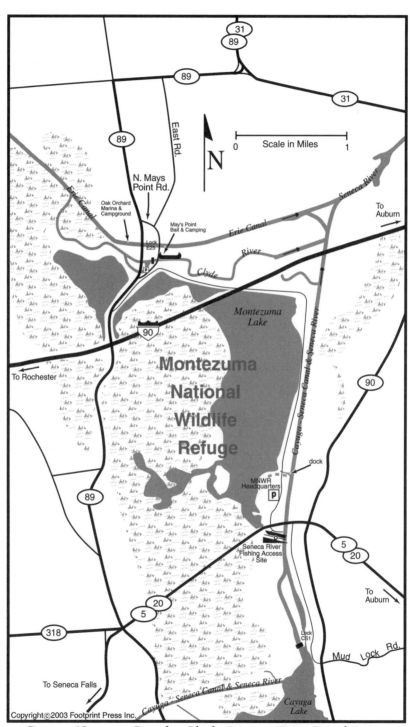

Cayuga/Seneca Canal - Clyde River - Erie Canal Loop

19

CAYUGA/SENECA CANAL
- CLYDE RIVER
- ERIE CANAL LOOP

Location: Montezuma National Wildlife Refuge, Seneca County

Directions: From I-90 take exit 41 (Seneca Falls) and head south on Route 414. Turn east onto Route 318 then east on Routes 5 & 20. Turn right at the DEC sign "Seneca River Fishing Access Site" across from the entrance to Montezuma Wildlife Management Area.

Launch & Take-out Site #1: Seneca River Fishing Access Site off Routes 5 & 20 has a large parking area and a sloped cement boat launch.

Launch & Take-out Site #2: May's Point Bait & Camping on Clyde River Drive below the dam has a cement ramp.

Best Season to Visit: Summer

Nearby Campgrounds: May's Point Bait & Camping, 3078 Clyde River Drive, Savannah, NY 13146, (315) 365-3183

Oak Orchard Marina & Campground, Route 89 at May's Point/Savannah, NY 13148 www.oakorchard.com, (315) 365-3000

Paddling Distance: 11.2 miles for the full loop (6.9 miles up the Cayuga/Seneca Canal to the Clyde River dam and back)

Down Cayuga-Seneca Canal to Clyde River: 2.5 miles
Up the Clyde River to the dam: 1.0 mile
Clyde River above dam to Erie Canal: 1.4 miles
Erie Canal to Lock 25: 1.0 mile
Lock 25 to Cayuga-Seneca Canal: 1.9 miles
Back up Cayuga-Seneca Canal: 2.5 miles

Estimated Time to Paddle: 5-6 hours for the full loop
4-5 hours up to the dam and back

Difficulty: ▬▬▬ (paddle to the May's Point dam and back)

▬▬▬ ▬▬▬ (paddle the loop, which includes 2 portages - bring gloves if you plan to lock-through)

Other Activities: Stopping on shore in Montezuma National Wildlife Refuge (along the Cayuga-Seneca Canal or Clyde

	River) is prohibited, but you can get out to rest or picnic at May's Point and at Lock 25.
	This is avid fishing territory. Try your luck at bass, carp and lake sturgeon.
Amenities:	May's Point Bait & Camping offers ice cream, lunches, picnic area, camping, cabins and outhouses.
	At Lock 25 there's a Porta-potty and picnic tables.
Dogs:	OK on leash
Admission:	Free
Contact:	New York State Canal Corporation
	1-800-4CANAL4, www.canals.state.ny.us

This route takes you north on the straight Cayuga-Seneca Canal through undeveloped Montezuma National Wildlife Area lands. Then, you'll turn west onto the winding Clyde River where mature forests line the banks and spill over into the waterway. But, being wide and deep, they offer no impediment. You'll be surrounded with the serenade of song birds (except for the few stretches near the Thruway where car noise will drowned out the birds). The Clyde River is dammed at May's Point. When the dam is closed the current will be barely perceptible. It can get strong when the dam is opened after heavy rains.

Turn around at the dam and retrace your path, or portage around it to continue on the Clyde River. Then turn right to enter the Erie Canal. At Lock 25 you can lock through or portage again. Beyond the lock, turn right to return to your starting point via the Cayuga-Seneca Canal.

Paddling Directions:

- From the Seneca River Fishing Access Site off Routes 5 & 20, head downstream in the Cayuga-Seneca Canal, quickly passing under the green metal superstructure bridge of Route 5 & 20.
- Pass a dock and canoe/kayak landing on the left. A trail leads to the visitor center, observation tower and public restrooms at Montezuma National Wildlife Refuge.
- Pass a small channel to the left. You can go explore it, but it will not provide access to Montezuma Lake.
- Pass small culverts, outflow from Montezuma Lake on the left. Fish were jumping here when we paddled in June.
- Pass another small dead-end channel to the left. You can explore it.
- Paddle under the noisy double bridge of the NY State Thruway (I-90).
- Quickly turn left into the Clyde River at the big sign "Welcome to the Cayuga-Seneca Canal." Notice that the water turns from green to brown.

- Follow the winding Clyde River through a thick forest and paddle around the many downed trees.
- When you see the first cottage, you'll also see the South May's Point Road bridge. Just beyond the bridge is the dam. Watch for the ramp to the right before the bridge and pull-out at May's Point Bait & Camping. Portage 100 yards across South Mays Point Road, past the dam and put in above the boom.
- Continue paddling upstream on the Clyde River, under the green metal Route 89 highway bridge.
- Reach the Erie Canal and turn right.
- Pass Oak Orchard Marina & Campground on your left.
- Pass under the green metal Route 89 highway bridge, then approach lock 25.
- You can lock through or exit via the metal stairs in the cement wall before the lock, portage 100 yards past the lock and re-enter via another metal stair below the lock.
- At buoy G547 turn right to enter the Cayuga-Seneca Canal.
- Paddle under the dual I-90 bridges and straight down the canal.
- After passing under the green Routes 5 & 20 bridge bear right to the original launch site.

Date visited:

Notes:

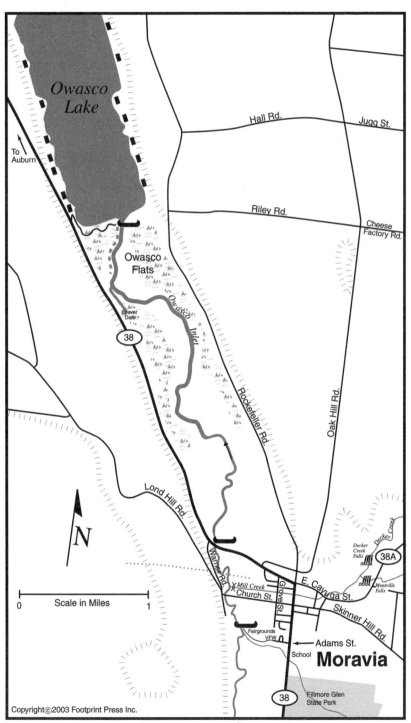

Owasco Inlet

20

OWASCO INLET

Location:	Moravia, Cayuga County
Directions:	From Route 38 in Moravia turn west on Adams Street at the VFW sign. Drive to the end of the street past the VFW Post and continue straight on the dirt road passing through the red vending buildings of the fairgrounds. At the end of the dirt road is a small circle for parking.
Launch Site #1:	At the back of the fairgrounds is an easy gravel slope to the creek.
Launch Site #2:	A dirt pull-off on the northeast side of the Route 38 bridge offers sloped grass to a large rock access area.
Take-out Site:	The Cayuga Parks & Trails launch where Owasco Inlet meets Owasco Lake. From Route 38 at the south end of Owasco Lake turn east on a road toward Cascades Restaurant. At the base of the hill, continue straight past two brown signs "Cayuga Parks & Trails" onto a gravel road. It will snake through Owasco Flats to the mouth of Owasco Inlet. Launching is via a sloped bank.

Put in + take out here!

Best Season to Visit: Early summer from Moravia
Anytime from the south end of Owasco Lake

Paddling Distance: 5.3 miles from Moravia to Owasco Lake
Fairgrounds to Route 38: 1.1 miles
Route 38 to Owasco Lake: 4.2 miles

Estimated Time to Paddle: 2-3 hours

Difficulty: (from the fairgrounds to Route 38 —fast flowing with sharp turns and strainers)
(from Owasco Lake upstream to Route 38)

Other Activities: Hike the 2-mile trail in Owasco Flats at the take-out

Amenities: The fairgrounds has a Porta-potty.
At the take-out is Cascades Restaurant. Also, South Shore Marina has a Porta-potty, groceries, a deli, and ice cream and rents canoes & kayaks, (315) 497-3006.

Dogs: OK

Admission:	Free
Contact:	Cayuga County Parks & Trails Commission
	Emerson Park, 6914 East Lake Road, Auburn, NY 13021
	www.co.cayuga.ny.us/parks/, (315) 253-5611

Welcome to Owasco Flats—a large fern and willow marsh and flood plain forest with Owasco Inlet running down its belly. It was also the original name of the town of Moravia. This fertile valley was cultivated by the Indians. Around 1850 a plank road was built across it, later replaced by the Lehigh Valley Railroad, which is now abandoned.

Paddling here is like encountering two distinct streams. From the fairgrounds in Moravia to the Route 38 bridge it's a narrow, fast-moving, windy stream with strainers at the bends. We waited for the slower water of July to paddle it and put up with a few pushes through shallow spots. Downstream of the Route 38 bridge we found shallows around islands and one easy portage over a downed tree, then the stream opened up to a wide, deep channel and the current disappeared. You paddle through a mature forest and at eye level with fields of ferns, watching the deer, muskrats, blue herons and beavers. One beaver circled our kayaks and slapped his tail repeatedly in warning. For an easy paddle all summer or fall long, launch at the south end of Owasco Lake and paddle upstream. You'll almost reach the Route 38 bridge before finding any impediments.

Paddling Directions:
- Head downstream from the fairgrounds. The stream alternates being shallow and deep and twists wildly.
- Pass under the green bridge of Lond Hill Road/Church Street.
- Mill Creek merges from the right, spanned by a red pedestrian bridge labeled "Finger Lakes Trail Runners."
- Pass under the brown Route 38 bridge. (Access is downstream, right.)
- Enter the Owasco Flats valley.
- Pass evidence of campers.
- The channel to the left can be explored for 10 minutes before it ends at a beaver dam.
- The take-out will be to the left when you reach Owasco Lake.

Date visited:

Notes:

Paddles in Onondaga, Oneida, Madison and Oswego Counties

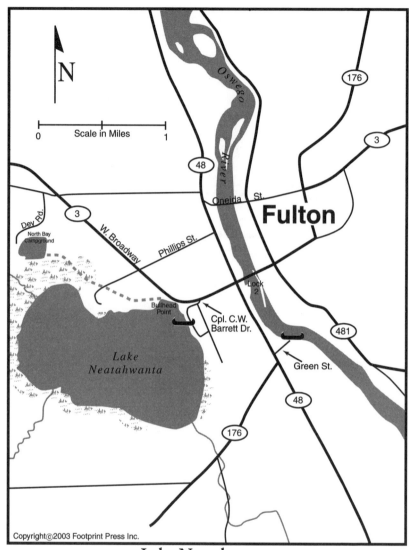

Lake Neatahwanta

21

LAKE NEATAHWANTA

Location: Fulton, Oswego County

Directions: In Fulton head west on Route 3 (West Broadway) over the Oswego River. As Route 3 bends, continue straight onto Cpl. C. W. Barrett Drive. It will bend left along the lake shore.

Launch and Take-out Site: Park along Cpl. C. W. Barrett Drive where there's a wide sloped gravel bank.

Best Season to Visit: Spring, summer and fall

Nearby Campgrounds: North Bay Campground, 40 North Bay, Fulton, NY 13069, (315) 592-2256

Paddling Distance: The lake is 1.5 miles wide

Estimated Time to Paddle: 1 - 2 hours

Difficulty: ▶━━● (wind may pose a challenge)

Other Activities: Hike (a 1-mile trail leads from the pier to North Bay Campground)

Amenities: Picnic tables & pavilions
Bullhead Point offers a large pier, a pavilion and Don's at Bullhead Point Restaurant with restrooms

Dogs: OK

Admission: Free

Contact: City of Fulton Recreation Office
141 South First Street, Fulton, NY 13069
(315) 592-2474

This is a large, open lake with wooded shores. The park at Bullhead Point offers a gazebo, pier and tourism center. Paddle a Thursday evening during the summer and you'll be serenaded by music from the Summer Concert Series.

Date visited:

Notes:

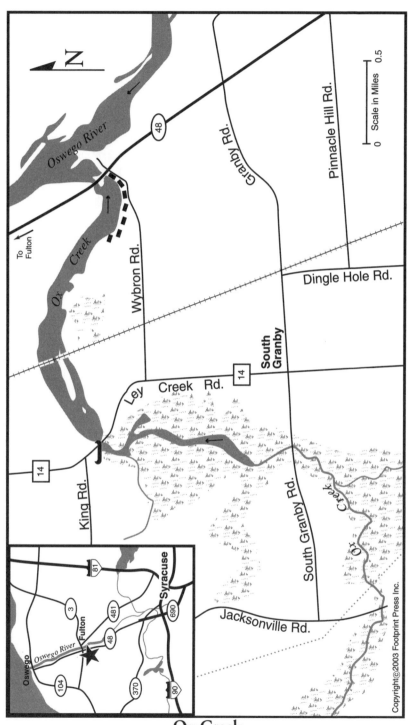

Ox Creek

22

OX CREEK

Location:	South Granby, Oswego County
Directions:	From Fulton head south on Route 48, then turn west on Wybron (or Wyborn) Road to the end. Turn north on County Route 14 (Ley Creek Road) to the bridge over Ox Creek. Park near the bridge.
Launch & Take-out Site :	From the County Route 14 bridge in South Granby, follow the short, easy sloped dirt trail upstream, left of the bridge (the SW corner) to launch.
Best Season to Visit:	Spring
Nearby Campgrounds:	North Bay Campgrounds, 925 Phillip Street Fulton, NY 13069, (315) 592-2256
Paddling Distance:	4 miles round trip downstream (to Oswego River) 2 miles round trip upstream (toward South Granby Road)
Estimated Time to Paddle:	2 hours round trip downstream 1 hour round trip upstream
Difficulty:	(negligible gradient)
Other Activities:	Fish, bird watch
Amenities:	None
Dogs:	OK
Admission:	Free

The dark, crystal-clear, tannin-stained water of Ox Creek can be paddled in any season—in theory. Lately it has become choked with water chestnut, an invasive aquatic weed, by late summer. This non-native plant came from Asia and was first recorded in North America in Massachusetts in 1859. It grows in an extremely dense mat that covers the water surface, making paddling difficult and preventing sunlight from reaching the native plants and fishes below the surface. Oswego County has been implementing mechanical harvesting and recruiting residents to do hand pulling to control this weed.

We paddled here in spring and found beautiful winding channels of water through bright green beds of arrowhead plants. Use the County Route 14 bridge as your launch and take-out points for forays both up and downstream on Ox Creek. Downstream you'll pass a few camps on a wide channel until you reach the Oswego River. Upstream you're heading through a winding channel into marshlands with abundant wildlife.

Lush beds of arrowhead plants line Ox Creek.

Downstream Paddling Directions (to Oswego River):
- From the Route 14 bridge, head downstream.
- At 0.7 mile pass through a tunnel under the Conrail tracks.
- Pass under the cement Route 48 bridge, left of the island.
- Reach the Oswego River. Turn around and head upstream on Ox Creek or see pages 97-98 for the take-out points downstream on the Oswego River.

Upstream Paddling Directions (toward South Granby Road):
- From the Route 14 bridge, head upstream.
- Enter cattails. You may encounter beaver dams.
- If the stream appears to end, follow the current through the trees.
- Turn around when you can no longer discern a channel or are impeded by low water, blow downs or beaver dams. It will be before the South Granby Road bridge.

Date visited:

Notes:

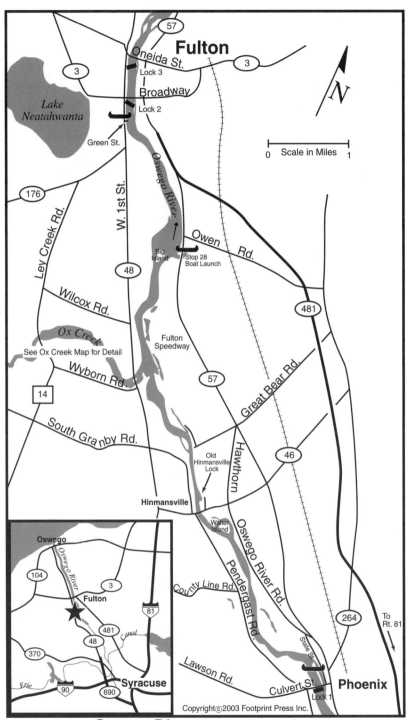

Oswego River (Phoenix to Fulton)

Fulton

Oneida St.
Lock 3
Broadway
Lock 2
Green St.

Lake Neatahwanta

176

Ley Creek Rd.

W. 1st St.

Oswego River

48

Wilcox Rd.

Ox Creek

See Ox Creek Map for Detail

14

Wyborn Rd.

South Granby Rd.

Big Island

Stop 28 Boat Launch

Owen Rd.

481

Fulton Speedway

57

Great Bear Rd.

46

Old Hinmansville Lock

Hawthorn

Hinmansville

Walter Island

Oswego River Rd.

County Line Rd.

Pendergast Rd.

Lawson Rd.

Culvert St.

State St.

Lock 1

264

To Rt. 81

Phoenix

N

0 Scale in Miles 1

Inset map:

Oswego

104

Oswego River

3

Fulton

81

481

Canal

48

370

Erie

90

690

Syracuse

★

23

OSWEGO RIVER
(Phoenix to Fulton)

Location:	Phoenix and Fulton, Oswego County
Directions:	From Route 81 north of Syracuse, exit onto Route 481 west. Exit onto Route 264 south. In Phoenix, turn right onto Culvert Street. Turn onto the island between the yellow liftbridge and the blue highway bridge. Park at the end.
Launch Site:	Launch from the end of the island below the yellow Culvert Street liftbridge. It's a nice sloped gravel bank.
Take-out Site #1:	A 15-car parking area and boat launch area off Route 57, labeled with a white sign "Stop 28 Boat Launch." There's a shallow gravel bank from which to launch or take-out.
Take-out Site #2:	City of Fulton boat launch off Route 48 at Green Street. There's no sign and very limited parking. It's a sloped asphalt ramp.

Best Season to Visit: Fall when the Erie Canal is closed.

Paddling Distance: 9 miles

Estimated Time to Paddle: 2 - 3 hours

Difficulty: (current can get strong, especially in spring)

Water Level Information: http://waterdata.usgs.gov/ny/nwis/rt (the gage, #04249000, is downstream from this segment at lock 7 in Oswego)

Other Activities:	Fish, bird watch
Amenities:	None
Dogs:	OK
Admission:	Free

The Oswego River is actually the Oswego Canal, a wide and deep 24-mile long channelized river with 7 locks and dams to control water levels and water flow. It connects the Erie Canal to Lake Ontario. Before this canal opened in 1828, the Oswego River had a 12-mile stretch of rapids and a significant waterfall called Oswego Falls. The first version of the Oswego Canal was 38 miles long, with 18 miles of river use and 20 miles of canals separated from the river by locks and dams. Small segments of the old canal channels still exist.

From May through mid-October this river is used by motor boats. You'll paddle past high, wooded banks with year-round homes. A few detours around islands will allow you to escape motor boat traffic periodically.

By late summer you may encounter water chestnut plants as a thick mat on the water in spots along Oswego River. This invasive, non-native weed is being removed by mechanical means and manual pulling. They are especially troublesome near Ox Creek.

Paddling Directions:
- From the island below Lock 1 in Phoenix, head downstream.
- In 3 miles, at buoy R32 bear right out of the main channel to circle around Walter Island.
- Bear right to continue downstream in the main Oswego River channel.
- Pass under the high green superstructure of the County Route 46 bridge.
- Watch on the right for remains of the old Hinmansville lock.
- For a side trip, bear right onto a section of the old Oswego Canal that parallels the current channel. You'll either have to reverse direction and paddle back to the Oswego River or portage to return.
- Ox Creek enters from the left (see page 94).
- After buoy R68 bear right in the main channel for the first take-out point or bear left to paddle through the shallower back channel around Big Island.
- After buoy G79, before the last building on the left, bear left to find the Green Street boat launch above the yellow Fulton dam. There is no sign, simply a sloped asphalt ramp.

Date visited:

Notes:

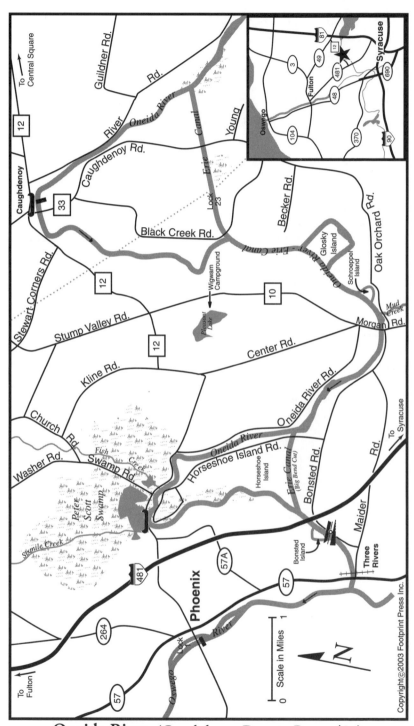

Oneida River (Caughdenoy Dam to Route 481)

24

ONEIDA RIVER
(Caughdenoy Dam to Route 481)

Location: Caughdenoy, Glosky Island, Horseshoe Island, Oswego/Onondaga County border

Directions: From Route 81, north of Syracuse, exit to Route 49. Head west on Route 49 to Central Square, then take Route 12 west to the lock and dam at Caughdenoy.

Launch Site #1: Launch below the dam at Caughdenoy. Parking is available below the dam on County Route 12. It's a sloped gravel launch. If the water's high, it may be turbulent at the launch site.

Launch Site #2: Along Oneida River Road at the north end of Horseshoe Island is a small parking area with access to the water from a bank.

Take-out Site: The DEC launch on Bonsted Street west of Route 481 has room for 20 cars and a sloped cement ramp under the dual Route 481 bridges.

Best Season to Visit: Fall when the Erie Canal is closed, so you encounter less motor boat traffic

Nearby Campgrounds: Wigwam Campground, RD#1, Pennellville, NY PO Box 1100, 13132, (315) 668-2074

Paddling Distance: Total distance: 13.4 miles
Caughdenoy to Erie Canal: 3.0 miles
Erie Canal/Oneida River junction west of Lock 23 to Morgan Road: 3.6 miles
Morgan Road to the start of Big Bend Cut: 1.7 miles
Oneida River from the eastern end of Big Bend Cut to Bonsted Street take-out (around Horseshoe Island): 5.1 miles

Estimated Time to Paddle: 6 - 8 hours

Difficulty: (negligible gradient)

Other Activities: Fish, bird watch
Amenities: None
Dogs: OK
Admission: Free

Portions of the Oneida River have been channelized to become the Erie Canal. The route described below uses side channels around islands rather than the direct route used by motor boats in the canal. Still, you may encounter motor boat traffic from May through mid-October in the official Erie Canal sections. You'll paddle through a mix of natural wooded areas, summer camps and year-round homes on a wide and deep channel. In spring and after heavy rains, the currents and eddies below Caughdenoy dam can be strong.

Paddling Directions:

- Head downstream from Caughdenoy dam, under the Caughdenoy Road bridge. You're in the original Oneida River, not the canalized portion yet.
- At 3 miles bear right at marker R168 onto the Erie Canal. (To the left is Erie Canal lock 23.)
- At marker G171A turn left to go around Glosky Island. (The Erie Canal continues straight.)
- Turn left to reenter the Erie Canal.
- At marker G179 turn left to go around Schroeppel Island. (The Erie Canal continues straight.)
- Turn left to reenter the Erie Canal.
- Mud Creek enters from the left. (You can paddle upstream on Mud Creek for several miles depending on the water level and prevalence of downed trees.)
- Watch for remains of the Oak Orchard Lock which dates back to the 1837 Oneida River/Erie Canal improvement.
- Pass under the Morgan Road (County Route 10) bridge. You've come 6.6 miles.
- At marker R200 (and the Pirates Cove Marina) bear right off the Erie Canal channel (away from Big Bend Cut). You're now heading north around Horseshoe Island.
- Bear left to stay near Horseshoe Island, passing Fish Creek to the right. (You can paddle under the low bridge to explore upstream a bit.)
- Bear left to stay near Horseshoe Island, passing a wide opening to Peter Scott Swamp and Sixmile Creek to the right. (You can paddle these areas. This is also the location of launch site #2.)
- Meet the Erie Canal (Big Bend Cut) again at marker R206 and bear right.
- Pass under the Route 481 bridge.
- Bear left for the take-out at the boat launch off Bonsted Street.

Note: You can continue another mile on the Oneida River, then turn right onto the Oswego River. Take out in two more miles above Lock #1 at Henley Park in Phoenix. This area is known for crosscurrents and can be dangerous.

Date visited:

Notes:

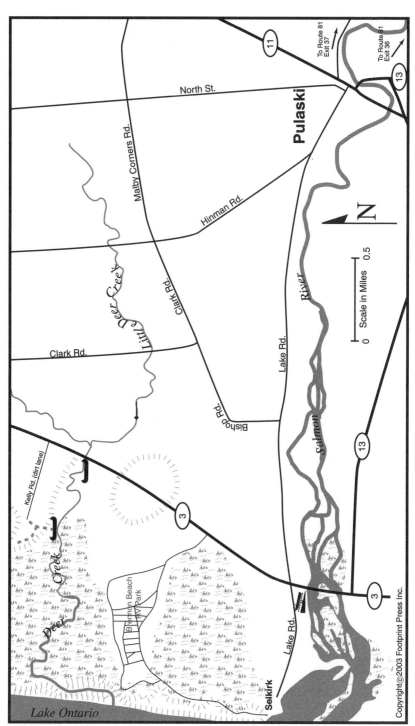

Deer Creek

25

DEER CREEK

Location: Pulaski, Oswego County

Directions: From I-81 take the Pulaski exit to Route 13 west. Turn north onto Route 3 and cross the Salmon River. Pass the Brennan Beach RV Park, then watch to the left for a DEC sign "Deer Creek Marsh Wildlife Management Area." Turn left into the parking area.

Launch and Take-out Site: From the DEC parking area a wide, mowed path leads past wooden posts for 100 yards to a flat but muddy launch bank. Or, follow the trail to the right into the woods and pass a steep bank. There will be a gradual slope to shore with big flat rocks from which to launch.

Alternate Launch: From the end of Kelly Road it's a long carry down an ATV track to the downstream launch spot.

Alternate Paddle: A motorboat launch on the north shore of Salmon River off Route 3 would allow you to explore the islands in Salmon River.

Best Season to Visit: Spring, summer or fall

Nearby Campgrounds: Brennan Beach RV Park, 80 Brennan Beach, Pulaski, NY 13142-9699, (888) 891-5979

Paddling Distance: 5.4 miles round trip

Estimated Time to Paddle: 2 -3 hours round trip

Difficulty: ▬◖ ▬◖

Other Activities: Fish, bird watch

Amenities: None

Dogs: OK

Admission: Free

Contact: DEC, Region 7
615 Erie Blvd. West, Syracuse, NY 13204-2400
(315) 426-7403, www.dec.state.ny.us/

Paddle west through Deer Creek Marsh, a flat plain with cattails to the right and woods to your left. By early summer the yellow water lilies and yellow irises will be in bloom. Watch for muskrat dens and turtles—they grow large here. As you approach Lake Ontario you'll sit low between sand dunes. Please stay off the sand dunes. They are fragile ecosystems that can

Deer Creek meets Lake Ontario.

be ruined by trampling. The channel into Lake Ontario may or may not be open, depending on recent winds and currents.

Paddling Directions:
- From the launch area, paddle downstream until the side channel merges into the main creek.
- At 0.7 mile you'll pass a sloped launch to the right. This might make a good picnic spot but not a good launch spot. Access to it from the end of Kelly Road is via an ATV track, not a driveable road.
- Continue down Deer Creek. Eventually the waterway will widen then swing south, parallel to Lake Ontario.
- Pass through the sand dune area and reach Lake Ontario at 2.7 miles. The trailers near the end are part of Brennan Beach RV Park.
- Return down the same channel to the launch site.

Date visited:

Notes:

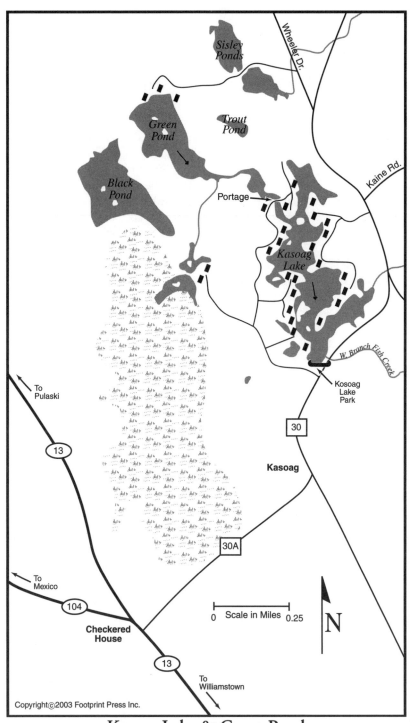

Kasoag Lake & Green Pond

26

KASOAG LAKE & GREEN POND

Location: Williamstown, Oswego County
Directions: Take I-81 north from Syracuse then Route 104 east. At Route 13 jog right then a quick left onto Route 30A. Turn left onto Route 30. Watch for a sign for "Kasoag Lake Park" on the left.
Launch and Take-out Site: The parking lot at Kasoag Lake Park offers a sloped gravel launch. Do not park on the grass and please let them know at the bar that you are parking while paddling.
Best Season to Visit: Spring, summer or fall
Nearby Campgrounds: Kasoag Lake Park, Route 30, Williamstown, (315) 964-2348 has cabins and a campground
Paddling Distance: Depending on where you go, you can do a 4-mile round trip
Estimated Time to Paddle: 1 - 2 hours
Difficulty: �━━● (in Kasoag Lake)

�━━● ▌━━● (to reach Green Pond requires a short portage over a roadway then over a beaver dam)
Other Activities: Fish
Amenities: Kasoag Lake Park has a bar and restaurant
Dogs: Not recommended
Admission: Free

Spring-fed Kasoag Lake has a convoluted shoreline dotted with small vintage cottages. Many of these have small docks with rowboats and canoes tied to them, so you may have company paddling. Kasoag Lake is connected to less populated Green Pond by a winding narrow channel. There's a lot to look at as you paddle the alcoves and small channels. You'll find lily-filled coves and little islands covered in pines.

Bring a fishing pole as these ponds are filled with perch, bass, bluegill and sunnies. In the upper reaches you may see beaver, muskrat, loons, ducks and herons.

Paddling Directions:
• Explore the shore of Kasoag Lake.

- At the northwest end, paddle upstream against the current into a channel.
- You'll probably have to do a short portage over a roadway. If the water's low you may be able to paddle through the culvert.
- You may encounter a beaver dam on the way to Green Pond. Portage over it and your reward will be a remote tree-lined pond.
- Return to the launch via a different shoreline.

Date visited:

Notes:

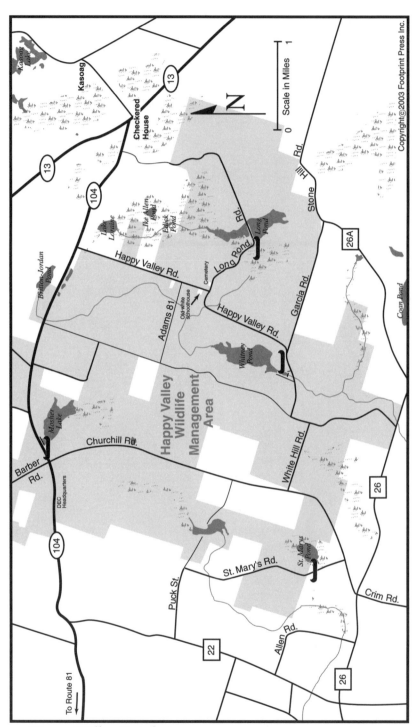

Happy Valley Ponds (St. Mary's, Mosher, Long Ponds and Whitney)

27

HAPPY VALLEY PONDS
(St. Mary's, Mosher, Long Ponds and Whitney)

Location:	Happy Valley Wildlife Management Area, Oswego County
Directions:	Take Route 104 east past Mexico. Or, exit from I-81 onto Route 104 and head east. The roads to each pond are rough dirt roads. Directions to each pond are listed below.

Best Season to Visit: Spring or summer (avoid fall hunting season)
Estimated Time to Paddle: An hour each
Difficulty: ⊢━━◖

Other Activities:	Fish, bird watch, hike
Amenities:	None
Dogs:	OK
Admission:	Free
Contact:	DEC, Region 7
	PO Box 1169, Fisher Avenue, Cortland, NY 13045
	www.dec.state.ny.us/

Once farmlands, the forests surrounding these 4 ponds are in various stages of regeneration. The lands were purchased from failing farms during the depression. In the late 1930s WPA and CCC crews planted conifers and built Mosher, Whitney and Long Ponds. All the ponds are in woodlands where the songs of birds will predominate.

St. Mary's Pond

Directions:	From Route 104 head south on County Route 22 then east on Puck Street. Turn right onto St. Mary's Road. The pond will appear on the left with a pull-off before its outlet crosses the road.

Launch & Take-out Site: The pull-off is a dirt loop with room for a few cars and a wide, sloped path to water level.
Paddling Distance: St. Mary's Pond is 0.3 mile long

St. Mary's Pond has sparkling clear rust-colored water with convoluted waterway channels through scrub brush islands.

Mosher Pond

Directions: The parking area is off Route 104 just east of the DEC headquarters and Churchill Road.

Launch & Take-out Site: The parking area has room for 8 cars and an easy bank for launching.

Paddling Distance: Mosher Pond is 1.1 miles long

Mosher Pond is created by a dam at the north end. It's a lily-covered pond with a few small islands, encased in woods.

Lily pads on Long Pond.

Long Pond

Directions: From Route 104 head south on Happy Valley Road.
There is no road sign, but the intersection is marked
with a brown DEC "Happy Valley WMA" sign. It's a
rough dirt road. At the "T" in 1.6 miles, turn left onto
Long Pond Road. In 0.7 mile there will be a small pull-
off area on the left before the pond. If you continue on
the road you will be on an earthen dike through the
middle of Long Pond.

Launch & Take-out Site: Across the road from the pull-off is an easy
sloped dirt launch.

Paddling Distance: Long Pond is 1 mile long

Long Pond has lots of islands and lily pads. You can paddle on both sides
of Long Pond Road to enjoy the wild, scenic views and clear, rust-colored
water. The small road near the launch ends at a turn-around at the outflow
dam.

Whitney Pond

Directions: From Route 104 head south on Happy Valley Road.
There is no road sign, but the intersection is marked
with a brown DEC "Happy Valley WMA" sign. It's a
rough dirt road. At the "T" in 1.6 miles, turn right for
another 1.5 miles. Turn right into a parking area before
the outflow creek.

Launch & Take-out Site: From the parking area it's a 25-yard carry to
put in from a grassy bank above the dam.

Paddling Distance: Whitney Pond is 0.9 mile long

Whitney Pond is a long pond set in a forested valley with a high dam at
the south end.

Date visited:

Notes:

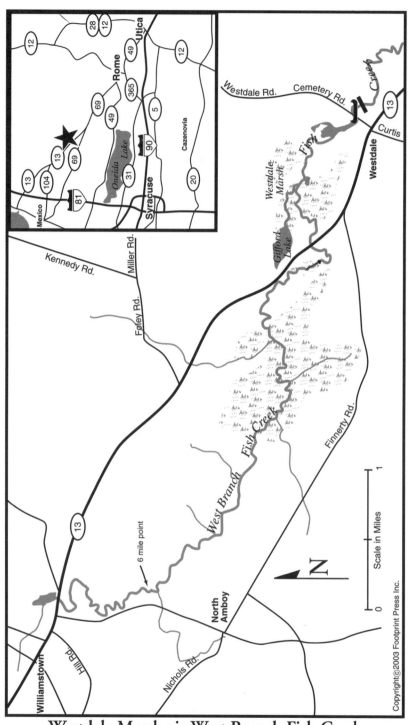

Westdale Marsh via West Branch Fish Creek

28

WESTDALE MARSH
via WEST BRANCH FISH CREEK

Location: Westdale, Oneida County

Directions: From Route 13 in Westdale, turn north onto Cemetery Road. The DEC parking area will be on the right before the creek marked with a brown and yellow sign "West Branch Fish Creek Public Fishing Stream."

Launch and Take-out Site: The DEC access site has room for 20 cars and wide wooden steps to water level.

Best Season to Visit: Summer

Paddling Distance: 1.7 miles from launch to the far end of Gifford Lake (one way)

1.4 miles from launch to Route 13 bridge via the left fork (one way)

Strong paddlers may be able to go 6 miles upstream

Estimated Time to Paddle: 2 hours round trip to Gifford Lake

6 - 8 hours round trip up West Branch Fish Creek

Difficulty:

Other Activities: Fish, bird watch

Amenities: None

Dogs: OK

Admission: Free

Contact: DEC, Region 6
207 Genesee Street, Utica, NY 13501
www.dec.state.ny.us/

Most of Fish Creek from Tug Hill Plateau to Oneida Lake is a bit rough for novice to intermediate paddlers. The East Branch is a wild white water ride and even much of the West Branch has rapids. This section through Westdale Marsh is the exception. Here the water slows and meanders endlessly through nooks, crannies, and bends, backed up by the Westdale dam.

The crystal clear water bears the rusty hue of tannin. Paddle upstream to explore undeveloped Gifford Lake or continue upstream in West Branch Fish Creek until beaver dams, downed trees or increasing current convince you to turn around and head back to the start.

Paddling Directions:

- Head upstream, under the Cemetery Road bridge. (Downstream is a dam.) Cottages and homes will dot the shore for the first 0.5 mile.
- Keep to the main channel. Watch the streambed to decipher the channel with the strongest current.
- In 1.5 mile the right channel leads to Gifford Lake.
- Bearing left will allow you to continue in West Branch Fish Creek to pass under the Route 13 bridge (0.6 mile after the junction) and continue upstream.

Date visited:

Notes:

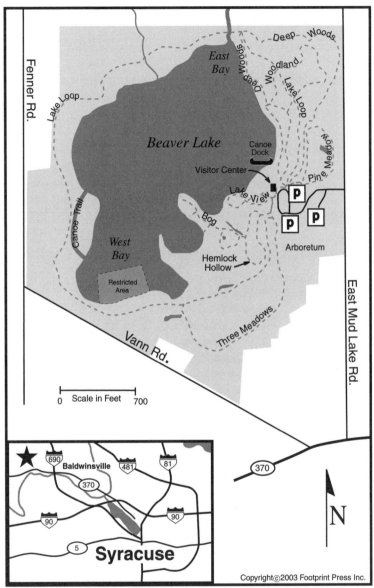

Beaver Lake

117

29

BEAVER LAKE

Location: Beaver Lake Nature Center, Baldwinsville, Onondaga County

Directions: From I-90 (exit 39) take Route 690 north to the second Baldwinsville exit. Head west on Route 370 for 2 miles and turn right (N) on East Mud Lake Road. The nature center entrance will be on the left.

Launch and Take-out Site: From the curb in front of the visitor center, it's a 200-yard carry to the canoe dock in east bay of the lake.

Best Season to Visit: Spring and summer

Paddling Distance: 2 mile loop

Estimated Time to Paddle: 2 hours

Difficulty:

Other Activities: Hike, attend workshops, bird watch

Amenities: Canoe rental, nature center has restrooms

Dogs: NOT allowed

Admission: $1.00 per vehicle

Contact: Onondaga County Parks
Beaver Lake Nature Center
8477 East Mud Lake Road, Baldwinsville, NY 13027
(315) 638-2519

Beaver Lake is a 650-acre park with a 9-mile network of trails and a 200-acre lake dedicated to discovery of the outdoors. Canoe rental ($8/hour) is available on a first-come, first-served basis at the visitor center, usually around mid-May to Labor Day. Be sure to call ahead about canoe times, regulations and when canoes are allowed on the water. The Beaver Lake canoeing season usually begins the second weekend of May for weekend paddling. Weekday paddling begins the last week of June. All paddling ends on Labor Day.

The park hosts over 400 workshops and events yearly. They include the spring Wildlife Art Weekend and the fall Golden Harvest Festival. The trails are open every day except Christmas, from 7:30 AM to dusk. (The visitor center opens at 8:00 AM). Bikes and motorized vehicles are not allowed on the trails. Pets, fires, collecting, fishing and swimming are prohibited at Beaver Lake.

The visitor center has taxidermy displays and a gift shop. This park was designed for family fun, and is truly a year-round outdoor hot spot. Its bird watching opportunities are exceptional on land and water.

The visitor center is handicapped accessible, and the Lakeview Trail is built to accommodate wheelchairs.

Paddling Directions:

- From the launch, you can paddle in any direction. If you paddle the lakeshore counterclockwise, look for the "Canoe Trail" entrance sign in the west bay.
- After exiting the canoe trail, cross the south end of the lake to explore the two southeast bays before completing the full circle back to the canoe dock.

Date visited:

Notes:

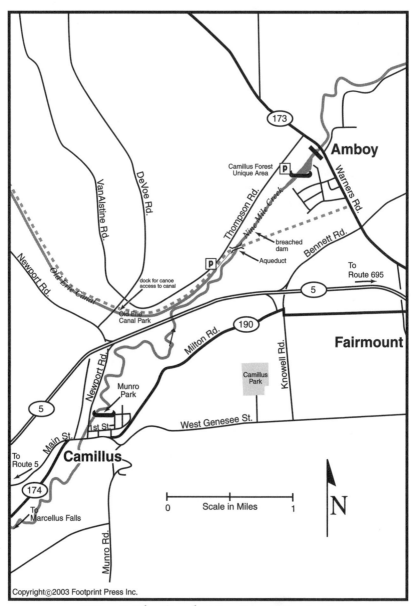

Nine Mile Creek (Camillus to Amboy)

NINE MILE CREEK
(Camillus to Amboy)

Location:	Camillus and Amboy, Onondaga County
Directions:	From Route 190 (Main Street, Camillus) turn north on Leroy Street. Pass 1st Street and continue into Munro Park. Drive to the northwest corner to a brown and yellow sign "Nine Mile Creek Erie Canal Water Trail."
Launch Site:	In Munro Park, from the water trail sign a path leads 50 yards to a wooden platform with wide, wooden steps into the water.
Take-out Site:	A parking area off Thompson Road (0.25 mile from Warners Road) is marked by a brown and yellow sign "Nine Mile Creek Erie Canal Water Trail." From the parking area a trail leads 175 yards across a field, into the woods, then down steps to a wooden platform with wide, wooden steps into the water.

Best Season to Visit: Summer

Paddling Distance: Total: 3.2 miles
        Munro Park to the aqueduct: 2.4 miles
        Aqueduct to take-out: 0.8 mile

Estimated Time to Paddle: 1.5 - 2 hours

Difficulty: (downed trees and a breached dam to run or portage)

Other Activities:	Bird watch, hike at Old Erie Canal Park or Camillus Forest Unique Area
Amenities:	None
Dogs:	OK
Admission:	Free
Contact:	DEC, Region 7 615 Erie Blvd. West, Syracuse, NY 13204-2400 (315) 426-7403, www.dec.state.ny.us/
	Munro Park (315) 487-3600

Paddling on Nine Mile Creek, under what once was
the Camillus Aqueduct on the Old Erie Canal.

The translucent green water of Nine Mile Creek is mostly deep and slow, providing a fun run from Camillus to above the dam in Amboy. A few shallow spots offer faster water and a few downed trees must be maneuvered around or over. There is a breached dam which offers a fast chute or a fairly easy portage along the right shore via a well-trodden path.

The grass-lined shores shelter abundant birds. The big attraction is paddling under the Nine Mile Creek Aqueduct, which once carried Erie Canal water over Nine Mile Creek. Old Erie Canal Park has plans for the future that include lining this aqueduct with timbers and refloating canal water across the aqueduct.

Paddling Directions:
- From Munro Park in Camillus, head downstream.
- Pass under two sets of power lines, then two more sets at a bend in the creek.
- Choose any of the 4 big culverts to paddle under Route 5. (The culverts are tall and wide and you can see light the entire passage.)
- Pass under the aqueduct after 2.4 miles. You will hear running water, but it's only a spillway from the canal into Nine Mile Creek. Your passage under the aqueduct is unobstructed.

- Shortly after the aqueduct is the breached dam. Pull out to the right to scope the channel or to portage around the dam.
- A few houses will appear on the right, then watch left for the wooden platform and steps—your take-out spot. (If you reach the dam, you went too far.)

Date visited:

Notes:

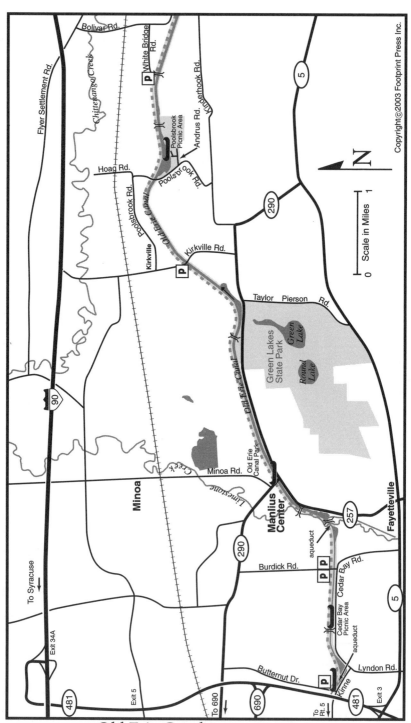

Old Erie Canal (start at DeWitt)

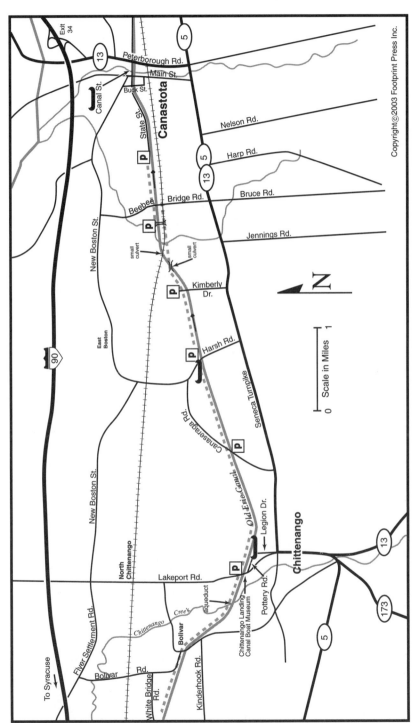

Old Erie Canal (end at Canastota)

31

OLD ERIE CANAL
(DeWitt to Canastota)

Location:	DeWitt, Fayetteville, Kirkville, Chittenango and Canastota, Onondaga County
Directions:	From Syracuse take Route 5 (East Erie Boulevard) east and turn left on Kinne Road. Just after the bridge over I-481, turn left onto Butternut Drive. Park to the right in the Old Erie Canal parking area.
Launch Site #1:	From the Old Erie Canal parking area off Butternut Drive, it's a short carry to a sloped grass launch area at the end of the canal channel.
Access Site #2:	A small parking area (not marked on the map) and sloped launch on Kinne Road near the corner of Cedar Bay Road.
Access Site #3:	A sloped gravel launch at Cedar Bay Picnic Area off Cedar Bay Road.
Access Site #4:	Old Erie Canal Park in Manlius Center off Minoa Road has cement step access.
Access Site #5:	A sloped gravel launch at Poolsbrook Picnic Area off Andrus Road.
Access Site #6:	The American Legion Park at the end of Legion Drive offers gravel steps to a nice launch area. (This is the last good take-out point before having to paddle through low, dark culverts.)
Access Site #7:	A 6-car parking lot at the Harsh Road bridge with water access upstream, left.
Access Site #8:	At the end of Kimberly Drive there's a parking lot on the north side of the canal with marginal water access downstream, right. (This is the last take-out to avoid the low culverts.)
Access Site #9:	Park along Canal Street in Canastota, near Peterborough Road. The canal ends at a sloped tile embankment.

Best Season to Visit: Spring, summer or fall

Nearby Campgrounds: Green Lakes State Park, 7900 Green Lakes Road, Fayetteville, NY 13066, (315) 637-6111
http://nysparks.state.ny.us/parks/

Paddling Distance: Total: 16.7 miles one way
Butternut Drive to Cedar Bay: 0.9 mile
Cedar Bay to Minoa Road: 2.1 miles
Minoa Road to Poolsbrook: 4.5 miles
Poolsbrook to Legion Drive: 3.3 miles
Legion Drive to Harsh Road: 2.4 miles
Harsh Road to Canal Street: 3.5 miles

Estimated Time to Paddle: Assuming roughly 2 miles/hour, the full route could take 9 - 12 hours

Difficulty: ▶━━━ (negligible current, could find downed trees, take out by Kimberly Road to avoid small culverts)

Other Activities: Bird watch, hike, bike (swimming is not allowed)
Chittenango Landing Canal Boat Museum, 7010 Lakeport Road, Chittenango, NY 13037 (315) 687-3801

Amenities: Cedar Bay Picnic Area has shelters, picnic tables, a drinking fountain, restrooms, a trail along the canal.
Poolsbrook Picnic Area has picnic tables and restrooms near the pedestrian bridge.
The American Legion Park has a pavilion, picnic tables, an outhouse and a baseball diamond.

Dogs: OK on leash

Admission: Free

Contact: Old Erie Canal State Historic Park
(315) 687-7821

A historical marker identifies the Old Erie Canal.

The 363-mile Erie Canal was opened with great ceremony in 1825. Dubbed variously "The Grand Canal," "Clinton's Folly," "Clinton's Ditch," and "The Big Ditch," the Erie Canal has been recognized as one of the great engineering feats of its day. With little technical knowledge or precedent to guide them, workers surveyed, blasted, and dug across New York State. They hewed through the hardest of solid rock, dug in infested marshes, devised and erected aqueducts to carry the canal across interrupting valleys and rivers, and constructed 83 locks to carry vessels through the variations in water height—one great set of locks rising nearly as high as the majestic falls of Niagara.

By connecting the Atlantic Ocean (via the Mohawk River) and the Great Lakes, the Erie Canal opened the West and initiated a great surge of commerce. Those were the glorious days of life at a snail's pace as horses and mules towed boats along the canal at four miles per hour taking just under six days to make the trip from Albany to Buffalo. The packet boats, dandy drivers with stovepipe hats, mule teams, and "hoggee" mule drivers are long gone. Today the Erie Canal and its towpath are used almost exclusively for recreation.

The canal was widened, deepened, and rerouted over the years to accommodate a succession of larger boats that hauled bigger loads. Initially, the canal was kept separate from creek waters by use of aqueducts and culverts. Later as engineering advanced, they learned how to control water levels in the canal and still merge it with natural waterways, such as the Seneca and

A narrow channel is available to paddle through the aqueduct over Limestone Creek.

Genesee Rivers. In 1917 the enhanced canal, called the Barge Canal, opened north of Syracuse and the segment you're about to paddle was abandoned; used only as a feeder to the new canal. In 1968 it became part of the New York State Parks System as a 36-mile-long linear park. The old towpath serves as a hiking/biking trail parallel to the waterway.

You will most likely not be alone on this paddle journey. The trail is popular with hikers and bicyclists and being near a metropolitan area, many paddlers ply these quiet waters also. For all its human use, you'll be surprised by the abundance and variety of wildlife. It's easy to paddle out and back since the easterly current is so slight. Or, enjoy a longer one-way trip. You'll paddle through aqueducts, pass a canal museum and go under bridges that give you an appreciation for the old canal cry "low bridge, everybody down!"

The Old Erie Canal continues past Canastota, through Durhamville and Higginsville to New London and it is paddleable. However, access at bridges is challenging because of steep banks and several difficult portages would be required. One is under the NYS Thruway. Another is in Durhamville where the canal ducks through narrow culverts under Routes 316 and 46, then again when the canal passes under Route 31.

Paddling Directions:
- From the end of the channel near Butternut Drive, paddle downstream toward the narrow aqueduct.
- The aqueduct will carry you over Butternut Creek then into a wide water area called Cedar Bay. (To the right is a 3-car parking area accessible from Kinne Road with a short carry to a beautiful, sloped dirt launch.)
- The bowstring truss bridge that spans the canal was built in 1886 and originally resided in the Canajoharie area. It was moved here in 1976 and now connects the hike/bike trail to Cedar Bay Picnic Area. (At the east end of Cedar Bay Picnic Area is a sloped gravel canoe launch.) This section of Clinton's Ditch was enlarged from 4 to 7 feet deep and from 40 to 70 feet wide between 1840 and 1850. Then in the 1890s it was deepened to 9 feet.
- Pass under the old cement and I-beam Burdick Road bridge.
- The canal will widen then narrow to a small trough as you pass through the aqueduct over Limestone Creek, then under a pedestrian bridge.
- Pass an old bridge (#4433200), blocked to traffic, then cement bridge abutments from an old railroad line.

Low Bridge - Everybody Down.
The Bolivar Road bridge spans the Old Erie Canal.

- Cross under the Route 290 bridge. You've come 3 miles. (To the left is a small park off Minoa Road with room for 20 cars. Cement steps lead from the water to a 20-yard carry down a paved sidewalk to the parking lot.)
- Pass under the footbridge that leads from the trail to Green Lakes State Park.
- Pass under the Kirkville Road bridge then the Poolsbrook Road bridge (#443240).
- To the right is the Poolsbrook Picnic Area with land access via a sloped gravel launch. Restrooms are shortly downstream near the wooden pedestrian bridge.
- Pass under the closed White Bridge Road bridge (#4424170).
- Pass under the cement Bolivar Road bridge (#4424160).
- Paddle through the aqueduct over Chittenango Creek. This one doesn't narrow to a trough like the previous two aqueducts.
- To your right will be Chittenango Landing Canal Boat Museum. Notice the dry dock area where boat repairs were completed.
- Paddle under the cement Lakeport Road bridge (#4424070).
- To the right will be gravel steps up to an American Legion Park.
- Pass under the Canaseraga Road bridge (#4424060).

- Pass under the Harsh Road bridge (#4424050). (There's a 6-car parking lot here with water access upstream, left.)
- Pass under the cement Kimberly Drive bridge (#4424150). (There's a parking lot on the north side of the canal with marginal water access downstream, right. Take out here if you want to avoid low culverts.)
- Pass through low, cement culverts under an old railroad grade then through another set under active railroad tracks.
- Pass under a cement bridge (#4424140). (Parking is available here with water access downstream, right.)
- Pass under the Beebe Bridge Road bridge (#4424130).
- Pass under the green-railed Buck Street bridge.
- The canal ends before Peterborough Road in Canastota. Take out via the sloped tile at the end of the waterway.

Date visited:

Notes:

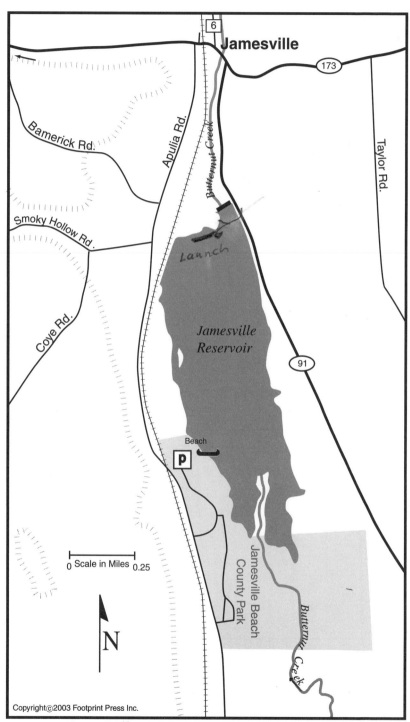

Jamesville Reservoir & Butternut Creek

32

JAMESVILLE RESERVOIR
& BUTTERNUT CREEK

Location:	Jamesville, Onondaga County
Directions:	From I-481 south of Syracuse, take Jamesville exit #2.
	Go south on Jamesville Road (Route 7) and south on
	North Street (Route 6) to Jamesville. Turn right onto
	Route 173 (E. Seneca Turnpike) then left onto Apulia
	Road. It's 1.5 mile to the Jamesville Beach County
	Park entrance.

[handwritten margin notes: NO, Rt. 91 — right in access road, by dam, left up to DEC site, fishing]

Launch & Take-out Site : From the lower parking area, carry to the right
of the beach for an easy launch.

Best Season to Visit: Spring, summer and fall

Nearby Campgrounds: Clark Reservation State Park, 6105 East Seneca
Turnpike, Jamesville, NY 13078, (315) 492-1590

[handwritten margin notes: lots of parking, kid army to reservoir]

Paddling Distance: 3.3-mile loop around the reservoir
1 mile up Butternut Creek (each way)

Estimated Time to Paddle: 2 hours around the reservoir
1 hour round trip up Butternut Creek

Difficulty:	⊢━ to ⊢━ ⊢━ ⊢
	(depending on wind level on the reservoir or how far up the creek channel you care to paddle)
Other Activities:	Hike, picnic, swim, fish, bird watch
Amenities:	Canoe and kayak rental, restrooms, picnic shelters, bathhouse
Dogs:	NOT allowed
Admission:	Beach open April - October, 9 AM - 8:30 PM, $4.25/vehicle admission, other times are free
Contact:	Onondaga County Parks, Jamesville Beach Park Apulia Road, Jamesville (315) 435-5252, jbeach@nysnet.ent

Butternut Creek flows north, filling Jamesville Reservoir, then Oneida
Lake on its way to Lake Ontario. The reservoir, with a dam at the north
end, is 1 mile long. At the southwest corner you'll find Jamesville Beach
County Park, a popular summertime fun spot for families. You can circumnavigate the reservoir (difficulty varies with the amount of wind) or
head south toward the marshy area. Here you'll find the channel of

Butternut Creek. Paddle upstream for about 1 mile or less, depending on how many blow downs you encounter or how hard you want to paddle against the increasing current.

Paddling Directions:
- Paddle anywhere you want in the reservoir, just avoid the dam at the northern end.
- For Butternut Creek, paddle toward the marshy area at the south end.
- The stream channel will be readily apparent.
- Paddle upstream until you run out of will, energy or patience with hauling over blow downs. Then head back downstream.

Date visited:

Notes:

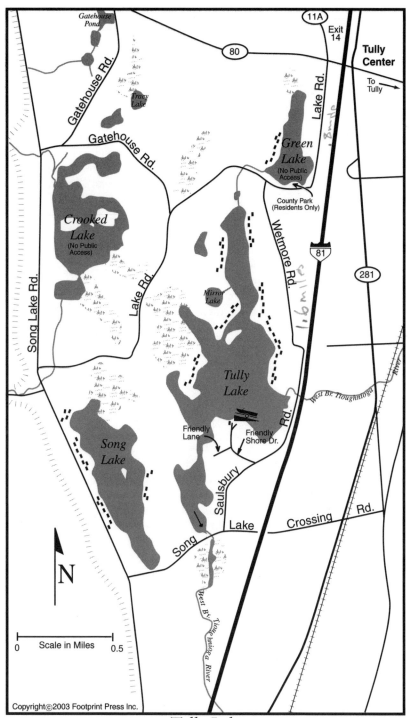

Tully Lake

33

TULLY LAKE

Location:	Town of Preble, Cortland County
Directions:	South of Syracuse, take Exit 14 west off Route 81 (Tully Center) and turn south onto Route 11A. Cross Route 80. You're now on Lake Road. Follow Lake Road around Green Lake (no public access) and turn left onto Wetmore Road. Continue south as Wetmore turns into Saulsbury Road. Turn right (NW) onto Friendly Shore Drive. The DEC parking area will be to the right at the end of this road.

Seems like you're getting back on 81.

Launch & Take-out Site: The DEC launch area onto Tully Lake has a sloped dirt launch and room for 15 cars.

Best Season to Visit: Spring, summer, and fall

Paddling Distance: Tully Lake is 1.8 miles long and 5.2 miles around

Estimated Time to Paddle: 2.5 - 3 hours around Tully Lake

Difficulty: ▬━━◄

Other Activities: Fishing

Amenities: None

Dogs: OK

Admission: Free

Contact: DEC, Region 7
615 Erie Blvd. West, Syracuse, NY 13204-2400
(315) 426-7403

Put In! Easy -20 ft

As the last of the great glaciers (the Wisconsin Glacier) retreated from Central New York, it paused near what is today the village of Tully and deposited a ridge of sand, gravel and till called the Valley Heads Moraine. Just south of the moraine it left six kettle hole lakes (Green, Tully, Crooked, Song, Tracy and Mud) and several ponds known collectively as Tully Lakes. The westernmost of these lakes were naturally landlocked, with no inlet or outlet, until the early 1800s when European settlers installed pipes to drain water for industrial use.

The eastern lakes (Green and Tully) have natural outlets at their southern ends. Green Lake flows into Tully Lake. The West Branch Tioughnioga River enters Tully Lake on its southeastern side and continues out the southern end. Today, the bridge over the Tully Lake outlet on Song Lake Crossing Road controls the level of Tully Lake during high-flow conditions, and a concrete weir maintains the Tully Lake level during low-water periods. The weir was built in the mid-1960s during a regional drought and is maintained by the Tully Lake Association, which places stop-logs across the weir during the late spring to maintain the lake level, and removes them in the early fall to lower the lake level.

Because they are landlocked and rely on rainfall and seepage, the average annual water-level fluctuations in the three western lakes ranges from about 2.5 to 6 feet. Water-level fluctuations in the eastern lakes average only about 1.5 feet because these lakes have natural outlets.

Another difference occurs too, due to their water source differences. Song Lake has soft water and Tully Lake has hard water. In Tully Lake, look for a cement-like deposit known as marl. Slowly over time, calcium leaches from glacially eroded limestone and calcium rich shales, seeps into the water and chemically reacts with bacteria, plankton, and organic matter to form a precipitate of calcium carbonate.

The lakes have been called various names over the years. Song Lake has been known as VanHousen Lake and Preble Lake. Tully Lake has been called Oserigooch, Susquehanna Lake, and Big Lake.

Legend has it that the Indians called Tully Lake 'Sacred Waters' and held it in great esteem. They would not allow "a fish to be taken from its crystal depths, nor a canoe to float upon its glassy surface." They considered an accidental drowning there to be a special desire of the Great Spirit.

Paddling Directions:
- Paddle anywhere you want on the lake. To the north, the shores of the island are posted private property. Mirror Lake is connected to Tully Lake via a small navigable channel, accessible under a low concrete bridge.
- The southern stretches are less populated. The southernmost end is blocked by the Song Lake Crossing bridge. Keep an eye out for turtles, muskrat lodges and patches of lilies.

Date visited:

Notes:

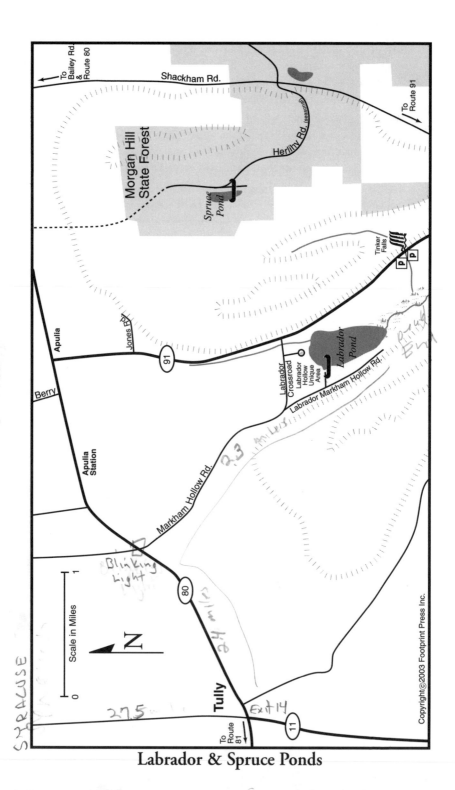

Labrador & Spruce Ponds

LABRADOR POND

Location:	Truxton, Onondaga County *Exit 14 – (take left – 2 miles)*
Directions:	Take the Tully Center exit off I-81 and head east on Route 80. In Apulia turn south *(rt.)* on Route 91. Turn right at the brown and yellow DEC sign for Labrador Hollow Unique Area onto Labrador Crossroad (it's unlabeled). At the end of this road, turn left onto Labrador Markham Hollow Road. Watch for another DEC sign marking the boat launch area on the left.

No — see map.

Launch and Take-out Site: The DEC boat launch area for Labrador Hollow Unique Area has parking for 6 cars next to a grass bank into a small side bay.

Best Season to Visit: Spring, summer and fall (fall would be beautiful)

Paddling Distance: The pond is 0.5 mile long.

Estimated Time to Paddle: An hour

Difficulty: ▬▬▬ (wind may pose a challenge)

Other Activities: Fish, bird watch

Amenities: Restroom and nature trail at the northern end of the pond

Dogs:	OK
Admission:	Free
Contact:	DEC, Region 7
	1285 Fishers Avenue, Cortland, NY 13045
	www.dec.state.ny.us/, (607) 753-3095

Put In: Easy – 20 ft

Labrador Pond is a natural glacial pond. It's tucked in a valley between steep wooded hills without a man-made structure in sight. The water is clear and lily pads cover sheltered bays. This is a delightful place for an escape to a natural environment.

Paddling Directions:
• Explore at will.

Date visited: 8/8/04

Notes: *Wind posed a challenge*
Nice hour paddle,
Lots of driftwood sculptures along lake

35

SPRUCE POND

Location: Fabius, Cortland County (see map on page 138)

Directions: Take the Tully Center exit off I-81 and head east on Route 80. Pass Route 91, then turn right onto Bailey Road. Bear right onto Shackham Road. Turn right onto Herlihy Road (it becomes a rough dirt road). Turn left at the "T" and the parking lot will be quickly to the right.

Launch and Take-out Site: The DEC parking area is labeled "Spruce Pond Fishing Access Site." It has an 8-car parking area with a short walk to a grass bank at the pond.

Best Season to Visit: Spring, summer and fall (fall would be beautiful)

Paddling Distance: The pond is small, only 20 by 100 yards

Estimated Time to Paddle: An hour

Difficulty: ▶━━◀

Other Activities: Fish, hike (the orange-blazed Onondaga Branch of the Finger Lakes Trail passes Spruce Pond)

Amenities: None

Dogs: OK

Admission: Free

Contact: DEC, Region 7
1285 Fishers Avenue, Cortland, NY 13045
www.dec.state.ny.us/, (607) 753-3095

Spruce Pond is man-made—formed by an earthen dam at the south end. It's dotted with tiny islands and surrounded by a dying pine forest on half of its shores. Bring your fishing pole as this pond is stocked with rainbow and brook trout.

Paddling Directions:
• Explore at will.

Date visited:

Notes:

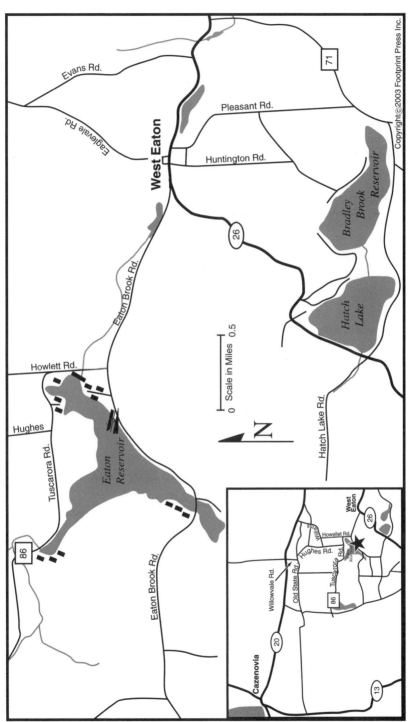

Eaton Reservoir

36

EATON RESERVOIR

Location: Eaton, Madison County

Directions: From Route 20, east of Cazenovia, turn south on Willowvale Road, then left (E) on Old State Road. Turn right (S) on Hughes Road. At the end turn left (E) on Tuscarora Road. At the end turn right on Howlett Road. Pass the dam of Eaton Reservoir. At the end turn right (W) onto Eaton Brook Road and watch for the yellow and brown DEC sign for "Eaton Brook Reservoir Fishing Access Site" on the right.

Launch and Take-out Site: Eaton Brook Reservoir Fishing Access Site offers plenty of parking, a sloped cement launch ramp and a small metal dock.

Best Season to Visit: Spring, summer and fall

Paddling Distance: The reservoir is 2 miles long

Estimated Time to Paddle: 2 - 3 hours

Difficulty: ▬▬◖ (wind may pose a challenge)

Other Activities: Fish

Amenities: None

Dogs: OK

Admission: Free

Contact: DEC, Region7
1285 Fisher Avenue., Cortland, NY 13045
www.dec.state.ny.us/, (607)753-3095

52-foot deep Eaton Reservoir is created by a high dam at the east end. It has three main branches of mostly wooded shores. Cottages are limited to a few spots. This reservoir is stocked with walleye and rainbow trout.

Ponds abound in this area of Madison County, but most are ringed with cottages and don't offer public access.

Paddling Directions:
• Explore at will

Date visited:

Notes:

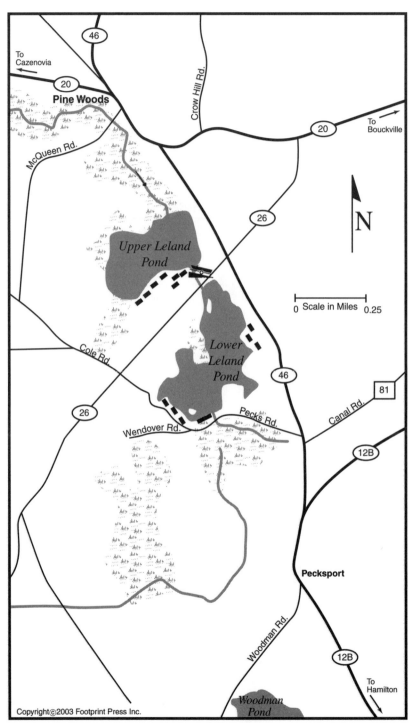

Leland Pond

37

LELAND POND

Location:	Town of Eaton, Madison County
Directions:	From Route 20, east of Morrisville, turn south on Route 46, then right (SW) on Route 26. The parking area will be on the right before the pond, marked by a brown DEC sign "Upper Lelands Pond."
Launch Site #1:	From the parking area you'll find a cement launch ramp and small metal dock.
Launch Site #2:	Across the road there's a gravel beach launch area.

Best Season to Visit: Spring, summer and fall.

Paddling Distance: 1.1 miles around Upper Leland Pond
2.9 miles around Lower Leland Pond

Estimated Time to Paddle: 0.5 - 1 hour around Upper Leland Pond
2 - 3 hours around Lower Leland Pond

Difficulty:	▸━━◣
Other Activities:	Fish
Amenities:	None
Dogs:	OK
Admission:	Free
Contact:	DEC, Region 7
	615 Erie Boulevard West, Syracuse, NY 13204-2400
	(315) 426-7403

Colonel Joshua Leland first settled in Eaton then later moved northeast, to what is today Leland's Pond. Just to the south, Josiah Peck and Alonzo Peck began their farm.

In October 1836, the Chenango Canal was completed, connecting the Erie Canal at Utica with the Susquehanna River at Binghamton. It was 97 miles long, 42 feet wide at top and 26 feet wide at the bottom, and 4 feet deep. There were 19 aqueducts, 52 culverts, 56 road bridges, 106 farm bridges, 53 feeder bridges, 21 waste weirs, 12 dams, and 11 lock houses, as well as 116 locks. The cost of the canal was $2,500,000, about twice what had been appropriated. The Chenango Canal operated from 1834 to 1876. During its short life, it cut freight shipping time between Binghamton and Albany to only four days as opposed to nine to thirteen days prior to that time.

Colonel Joshua Leland's ponds became a reservoir, supplying water for the canal. Josiah and Alonzo Peck eventually expanded the waterway area near their farm and formed what was known as Peck's Port, the busiest port on the Chenango Canal, handling the goods produced in Eaton. Today you'll find it on the map as Pecksport.

Leland Pond covers 96 acres with a maximum depth of 50 feet. The south end is created by an earthen dike. Paddle the marshy areas at the far ends and around several small islands. Its shores contain a few scattered cottages but are mostly woods and marshes. The launch site is labeled "no swimming."

The pond is bisected by Route 26. In 1896 a causeway was built through the pond to support the Pecksport Connecting Railway (part of the New York, Ontario & Western Railway) as a 3.8 mile link between the O. & W. mainline at Whites Corners with O. & W.'s Utica Branch at Pecksport. It was built through the pond to avoid the heavy grade over Eaton Summit (elevation 1,320 feet).

The culvert under Route 26 is 2 feet high and would be difficult to paddle through. Instead, carry your canoe or kayak across to enjoy both sections of this pond.

Paddling Directions:
  • Explore at will.

Date visited:

Notes:

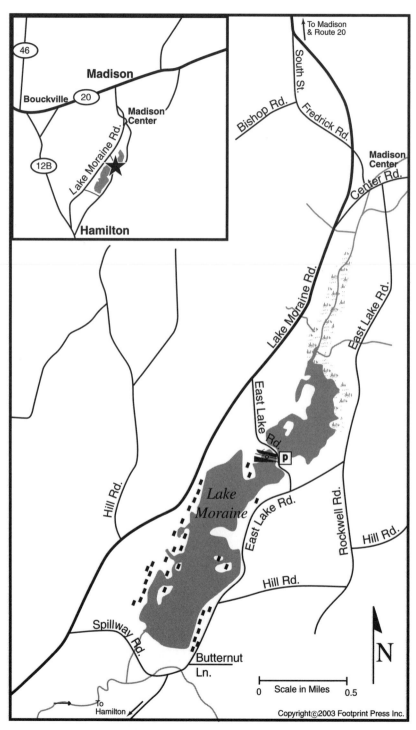

Lake Moraine (Madison Reservoir)

38

LAKE MORAINE
(Madison Reservoir)

Location: Town of Madison, Madison County

Directions: From Route 20, in Madison, turn south on South Street, then left (SE) on Lake Moraine Road. Cross Frederick Road and Center Road, then turn left onto East Lake Road. The parking area will be on the left, between the lakes, marked by a brown DEC sign "Madison Reservoir."

Launch & Take-out Site #1: From the parking area you'll find a sloped gravel launch ramp.

Launch & Take-out Site #2: Across the road there's a sloped cement launch and a small metal dock.

Best Season to Visit: Spring, summer and fall

Paddling Distance: From the launch it's 0.6 mile to the northern end and 1.2 miles to the southern end of the lake.

Estimated Time to Paddle: 1 - 2 hours

Difficulty:

Other Activities: Swim, fish

Amenities: None

Dogs: OK

Admission: Free

Contact: DEC, Region 7
615 Erie Blvd. West, Syracuse, NY 13204-2400
(315) 426-7403

Lake Moraine (a.k.a. Madison Reservoir) was created in 1837 as a feeder reservoir for the Chenango Canal. See page 144 for the history of the canal. Lake Moraine covers 250 acres with a maximum depth of 46 feet. The southern section of this lake is ringed with cottages and their associated motor boats. The northern lake is more natural and quiet. Have fun exploring its marshy edges and paddling around the island. If you take a fishing pole, you can fish for largemouth bass, pickerel and crappies.

Date visited:

Notes:

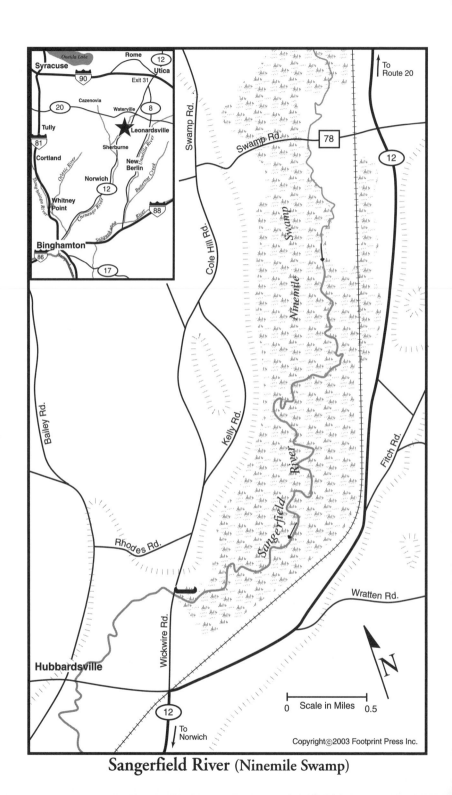

Sangerfield River (Ninemile Swamp)

39

SANGERFIELD RIVER
(Ninemile Swamp)

Location: Hubbardsville, Madison County
Directions: From Route 20 (south of Waterville), turn south onto Route 12. (Or, head north on Route 12 from Norwich.) Turn northeast onto Wickwire Road near Hubbardsville. Cross the railroad tracks and park at the pull-off at the bridge over the Sangerfield River.
Launch and Take-out Site: Follow the well-established dirt ramp to launch from the sloping grassy shore at either side of the Wickwire Road bridge over the Sangerfield River. There's room for several cars to park here.
Best Season to Visit: Spring, summer or fall
Paddling Distance: Total distance: approximately 6 miles round trip
Wickwire Road to Swamp Road: 4.6 miles
Estimated Time to Paddle: 4 hours round trip
Difficulty: (paddle against current, downed trees)
Other Activities: Bird watch
Amenities: None
Dogs: OK
Admission: Free

From Wickwire Road you'll be paddling upstream toward Swamp Road. It is possible to put in at Swamp Road and paddle downstream, but you're likely to encounter many downed trees and barbed wire across the stream just below Swamp Road. Instead, launch at Wickwire Road and paddle upstream until the challenge imposed by the impediments reaches your threshold, then return downstream to the launch point. Downstream from Wickwire Road is highly impeded, so it's not recommended for paddling.

Despite these challenges, this is a popular route. Ninemile Swamp is filled with beavers, great blue herons, green herons, a variety of other birds, many wildflowers and flowering shrubs. The current is usually slow-moving, flat water, except in spring run off or after a heavy rain, making this an easy paddle for beginners. Paddling round-trip from a single point means you don't have to bother spotting a car at the take-out.

At high water you may be boat-bound. In lower water conditions such as summer, you can probably picnic on the grassy shores. This is a swamp, but you'll also find an abundance of large trees.

Legend has it that the notorious Loomis Gang used Ninemile Swamp as a hideout in the 1800s. They eluded lawmen in the swamp after stealing horses, painting them and selling them to the US Army. Parts of the legend have them keeping human captives and setting barn fires. If you can find a copy, read *The Loomis Gang* by George W. Walter (published 1953) before heading out to paddle this swamp.

Paddling Directions:

(don't go under bridge.)

- From the Wickwire Road launch, head upstream.
- The waterway will eventually narrow.
- Paddle until you tire of dealing with downed trees, beaver dams and/or barbed wire, then turn around and head back downstream to Wickwire Road.

Date visited: 9/4/17

Notes:

1.5 hrs from Camillus, put Wickwire Rd, Hubbardsville, NY in GPS.

Great parking + easy put in.

No invasive weeds; obstruction about 2.5 miles in, could be portaged, or cut path thru, 2-3 pee places easily accessible ~ 2 miles in. Silty bottom, 1 heron, several ducks, very nice paddle, wish it was closer though,

Paddles in Cortland, Chenango and Broome Counties

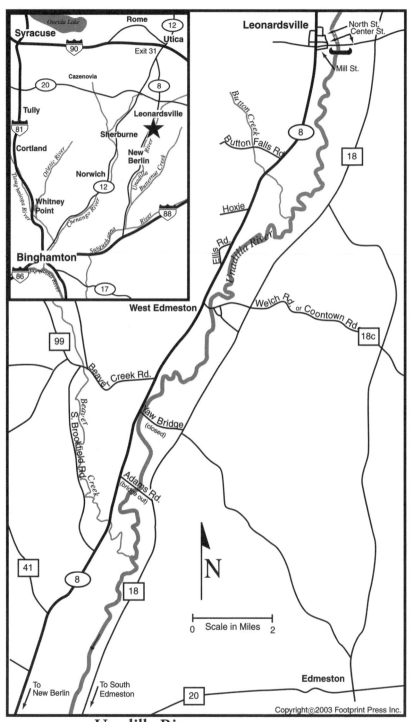

Unadilla River (start at Leonardsville)

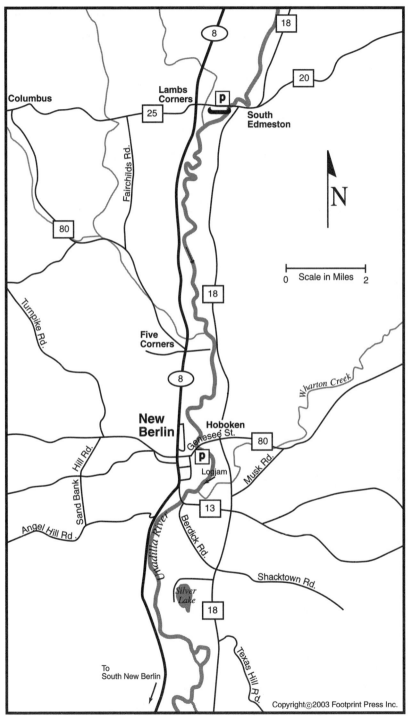

Unadilla River (middle through New Berlin)

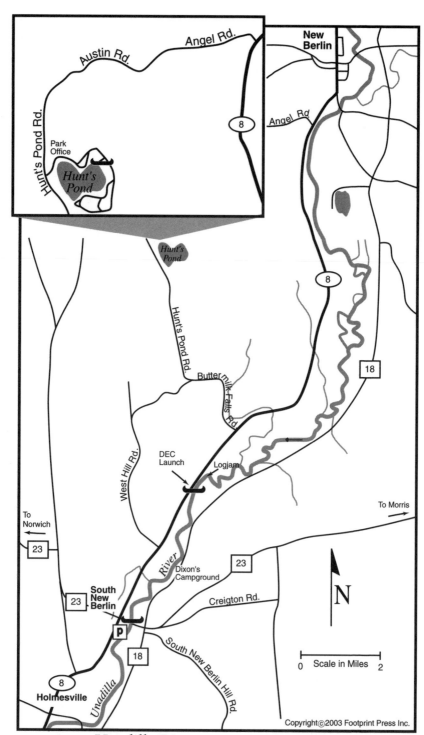

Unadilla River (end at South New Berlin)

40

UNADILLA RIVER
(Leonardsville to South New Berlin)

Location:	Madison and Chenango Counties on the border of Otsego County
Directions:	Take Route 8 south from Utica. Pass Route 20 and continue south on Route 8 to Leonardsville. In Leonardsville take the third left onto Center Street. There is a grassy pull-off area near the bridge.
Launch Site #1:	From the Center Street bridge in Leonardsville, carry over the guardrails to launch upstream right. This side presents a grassy, less steep access.
Low Water Launch Site:	Begin at South Edmeston where County Routes 20 & 25 meet at the county line. You have to park along the road and carry to the downstream, left side.
Take-out Site #1:	A DEC access site with parking for 8 cars and a hand launch is on the east side of Route 8 between West Hill Road and Buttermilk Falls Road.
Take-out Site #2:	The DEC "South New Berlin Fishing Access" parking area on County Route 23 in South New Berlin offers parking for 10 cars and sloped grassy access with wooden steps.
Best Season to Visit:	April to June or after a heavy rain
Nearby Campgrounds:	Dixon's Riverside Memorial Campground North East River Road, South New Berlin, 13843 (607) 859-2584
Paddling Distance:	Total: 32 miles Leonardsville to West Edmeston: 10 miles (4 hours) West Edmeston to South Edmeston: 7 miles (3 hours) South Edmeston to New Berlin: 5 miles (2.5 hours) New Berlin to South New Berlin: 10 miles (5 hours)
Estimated Time to Paddle:	Approximately 13 hours
Difficulty:	(3.5 feet per mile gradient, maneuver around tires, sharp bends and downed trees)
Other Activities:	Fish, bird watch
Amenities:	None
Dogs:	OK

Admission:	Free
Contact:	A comprehensive "Unadilla River Canoe Guide" can be purchased from Rogers Environmental Education Center (PO Box 716, Sherburne, NY 13460-0716, phone (607) 674-4017) for $2 plus postage.

This river of many bends, winds through a wide valley and forms the county border between Madison and Otsego at its northern reaches and Chenango and Otsego at the lower portions. The section below Leonardsville was shallow moving water with lots of ripples in September but was deep enough to paddle. It can be quite fast in spring runoff. From Leonardsville to New Berlin, the water is generally clear as it wanders past a mixture of fields and farmland. In the low water conditions of summer you may need to drag your boat over some sections. This river was once free of debris, but now is strewn with tires, evidence of a flood that ravaged a tire dump. The worst of the tires range from West Edmeston to New Berlin.

Plan a shorter trip if there's a strong south or southwest wind. Otherwise, this trip will feel like it lasts forever. Below New Berlin the river is wide and deep. It divides around numerous islands and you have to choose carefully to find the channel with the greatest water flow and least blockage by downed trees. There are two logjams to portage over south of New Berlin. Beyond the section described here (downstream from South New Berlin), you'll encounter rapids and class II water.

Paddling Directions:
- Head downstream from Leonardsville.
- In West Edmeston, pass a cement bridge with silver metal rails (Welsh Road). (Parking along the road is marginal, access is downstream, left.)
- Next comes a rusted old metal and wooden bridge that is closed to traffic on Yaw Bridge Road. A plaque on the bridge reads "W'ght Iron Bridge Co., Canton, O." (Access is upstream, left, which means vehicles must approach Yaw Bridge Road from the east.)
- Shortly pass the abutment for what used to be Adams Road bridge. (Access from the east on Adams Road provides good parking at the end of the road with river access downstream, right.)
- Beaver Creek comes in from the right.
- In South Edmeston the bridge (County Route 20/25) is cement with silver rails. (Access is downstream, left.)

- Enjoy a remote stretch—devoid of man-made structures—with abundant sunshine.
- When buildings appear, you're nearing New Berlin. Pass under a cement bridge with brown beams and silver rails. (River access is upstream, right. Park at Parts Plus Auto Parts off Genesee Street.)
- Enjoy the cover of black willow trees arching over the waterway.
- 0.75 mile below the Genesee Street/Route 80 bridge is the first log-jam to portage around.
- Wharton Creek comes in from the left shortly before the green metal bridge of County Route 13 in New Berlin.
- The river splits around several large islands.
- 0.25 mile before the DEC launch site is the second logjam to portage around.
- Pass a DEC access site with parking for 8 cars and a hand launch on the right.
- Bear downstream, right for take-out at the County Route 23 bridge at South New Berlin.

Date visited:

Notes:

41

HUNT'S POND

Location: Hunt's Pond State Park, New Berlin, Chenango County (see map on page 154)

Directions: From Utica, head south on Route 8 through New Berlin. Turn right onto Angel Road and bear left as it becomes Austin Road, then Hunt's Pond Road. Watch on the left for a brown and white sign "Hunt's Pond."

Launch & Take-out Site: A gradually sloped launch at the parking area

Best Season to Visit: Spring, summer and fall

Nearby Campgrounds: Hunt's Pond State Park offers primitive camping in secluded sites with picnic tables. Register at the park office, 4-8 PM.

Paddling Distance: It's 0.3 mile across the pond.

Estimated Time to Paddle: 0.5 hour

Difficulty: ▶━━◼

Other Activities: Fish, picnic, camp (call 1-800-456-CAMP to reserve a campsite)

Amenities: Restrooms (clean chemical toilets, no showers), canoe and kayak rentals

Dogs: OK on leash

Admission: $5/week or $15/season

Restrictions: Only hard bottom boats, kayaks or canoes are permitted. Canvas, rubber or plastic rafts, sailboats and windsurfers are not allowed.

Contact: Hunt's Pond State Park
452 Hunt's Pond Road, New Berlin, NY 13411-2716
(607) 859-2249

50-acre Hunt's Pond sits in a glacially formed basin and has a pristine treed shoreline and lily patches along the edges. It has abundant alcoves in which to poke about. Hunt's Pond State Park covers 250 acres and is adjacent to 1,100 acres of state forest land. DEC acquired the land in 1962 from Adrian and Mildred Hunt. It became a state park in 1976.

Date visited:

Notes:

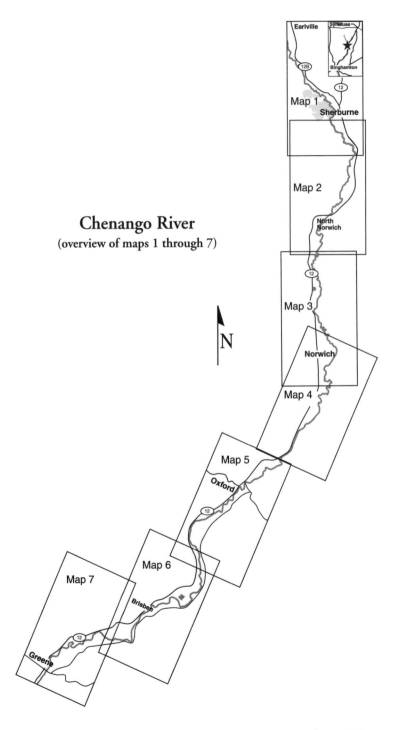

Chenango River
(overview of maps 1 through 7)

N

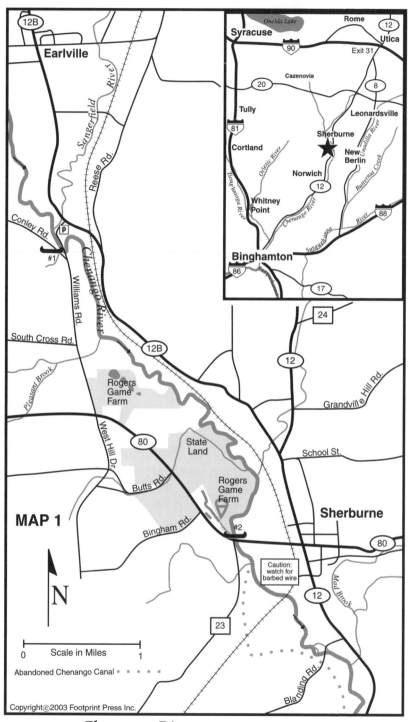

Chenango River (start south of Earlville)

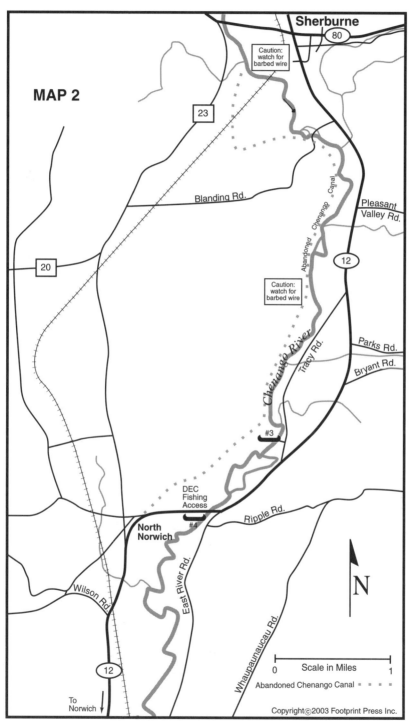

MAP 2

Sherburne

Caution: watch for barbed wire

23

Blanding Rd.

20

Pleasant Valley Rd.

Abandoned Chenango Canal

12

Caution: watch for barbed wire

Chenango River

Parks Rd.

Tracy Rd.

Bryant Rd.

#3

DEC Fishing Access

Ripple Rd.

North Norwich

#4

East River Rd.

Wilson Rd.

Whaupaunaucau Rd.

N

0   Scale in Miles   1

Abandoned Chenango Canal • • • • •

12

To Norwich ↓

Copyright©2003 Footprint Press Inc.

Chenango River (middle through North Norwich)

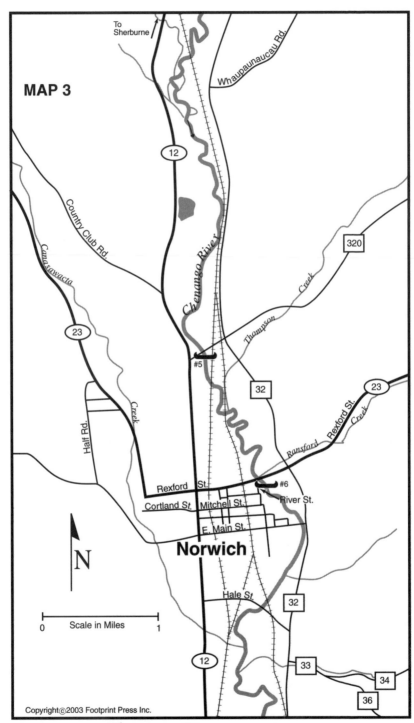

MAP 3

To Sherburne

Whaupaunaucau Rd.

Chenango River

Country Club Rd.

Canasawacta

12

320

Thompson Creek

23

#5

32

23

Half Rd.

Creek

Ransford

Rexford St.

Creek

Rexford St. #6

River St.

Cortland St.   Mitchell St.

E. Main St.

Norwich

N

Hale St.

32

0   Scale in Miles   1

12

33

34

36

Chenango River (end at Norwich)

42

CHENANGO RIVER
(Earlville to Norwich, maps #1 - #3)

Location:	Earlville, Sherburne, North Norwich and Norwich, Chenango County (See the overall map on page 159 and the inset map on page 160.)
Directions:	From Route 12 just north of Sherburne, take Route 12B north. Turn left (S) onto Williams Road. Pass a DEC fishing access parking area, then cross over the Chenango River. Immediately turn right (W) onto Conley Road. Park in the pull-off area along Conley.
Launch Site #1:	From Conley Road, south of Earlville, there is a beautiful, sloped grass launch area.
Launch Site #2:	West of Sherburne, on the north side of Route 80 is a DEC parking area with two tiers of parking and a 40-yard carry to a flat gravel launch area.
Launch Site #3:	A dirt road off Tracy Road leads to old bridge abutments and an easy launch site.
Launch Site #4:	A DEC fishing access site with parking for 16 cars and a sloped, mowed grass launch is off Route 12 in North Norwich.
Launch Site #5:	From Route 12 north of Norwich, turn east onto County Route 320. Park in the lot behind BSB Bank & Trust. A 10-yard carry down sloped gravel leads to water access downstream, right of the bridge.
Take-out Site #6:	From Route 12 in Norwich, turn east onto Route 23. Immediately before the Chenango River bridge, turn right onto River Street. On the left will be Kiwanis Park with a 12-car parking area and river access.

Best Season to Visit: Spring (except flood stage), summer and fall

Paddling Distance: Total: 20.0 miles

Conley Road to Route 80: 4.6 miles (2 hours)
Route 80 to Tracy Road: 5.2 miles (2 hours)
Tracy Road to Route 12: 1.3 miles (0.5 hour)
Route 12 to Route 320: 6.9 miles (2.5 hours)
Route 320 to River Street: 2.0 miles (0.75 hour)

Estimated Time to Paddle: 7-8 hours

Difficulty: (moderately moving current, 4.2 feet per mile gradient, some barbed wire across the stream)

Water Level Information: http://waterdata.usgs.gov/ny/nwis/rt (the gage, #01505000, is at Sherburne, within this segment)

Other Activities: Fish, bird watch hike at Rogers Environmental Conservation Center

Amenities: Kiwanis Park at the take-out has picnic tables, pavilions, grills, and a playground

Dogs: OK

Admission: Free

Contact: A comprehensive "Chenango River Canoe Guide" can be purchased from Rogers Environmental Education Center (PO Box 716, Sherburne, NY 13460-0716, phone (607) 674-4017) for $2 plus postage.

The Chenango River comes to life in a swamp near Morrisville in Madison County and flows south for 119 miles through the Chenango Valley to join the Susquehanna River in Binghamton. Its average gradient is less than 4 feet per mile, making it one of the most gently sloping streams in New York State. Because of this, water takes a while to make its way into the river and takes its time leaving. Therefore, high water occurs 2 to 3 days after a heavy rain. Most of the river is canoeable with over 70 miles devoid of dams, waterfalls or rapids.

At the launch site off Conley Road, the Chenango River was deep, 50 feet wide and had a gentle current in September. We've heard of launching upstream from the Middleport Road bridge in Randelsville, but we found this northerly stretch to be too shallow and have heard that it has trees and barbed wire across the water and is littered with garbage and junk cars— not very appealing.

Downstream from Earlville, it's a tree-shaded waterway, which means its cool in summer. Beware of potential downed trees at some of the sharp bends. You're likely to see flocks of geese and ducks, deer, otter and beaver that make the Rogers Environmental Conservation Center near Sherburne their home. The Rogers Environmental Conservation Center lands are a good place to get out for a picnic or to stretch your legs on some trails.

The paddling directions for this segment end at the River Street, Norwich, take-out. You can continue south through Norwich (The maps cover the entire 7.2 -mile route from River Street to Halfway House bridge. See map on page 167.), but the section from River Street to Halfway House bridge is urban and littered. A rural section picks up again below Halfway House bridge. That's where paddling segment #43 begins (see page 171).

Paddling Directions:

- From the Conley Road launch site (#1), head downstream under the green metal Williams Road bridge.
- To your left will be the Delaware, Lackawanna and Western Railroad line and the abandoned Chenango Canal.
- You'll pass two parcels of Rogers Environmental Conservation Center lands on your right.
- Pass under an old green railroad bridge and right behind it the low silver bridge of Route 80. Notice some old pilings from a previous bridge at a bend in the river. (A gravel bar makes a nice launch or take-out spot. But, it's only 40 yards to the DEC parking area (#2) off Route 80.)
- Keep an eye out for barbed wire across the river. There's one just south of Route 80 and another mid-way to North Norwich. They're used for cattle crossings.
- Pass under a Delaware, Lackawanna and Western Railroad bridge.
- Pass under the green metal Blanding Road bridge.
- The river splits around an island.
- Watch to the right to see an intact section of the abandoned Chenango Canal bed.
- Hand-laid stone abutments along shore signal a bridge that is no longer there. (Upstream, left is an easy launch area (#3). Access is from a dirt road off Tracy Road.)
- Shortly after the abutments is a large island.
- Next is the silver highway bridge of Route 12 in North Norwich. (Downstream, right is a sloped, mowed grass launch (#4) with a 10-yard carry to the DEC "Chenango River Fishing Access Site" with parking for 16 cars.)
- Watch for overhead power lines.
- Pass under paired railroad bridges. One is for the Delaware, Lackawanna and Western Railroad. The other carries the Ontario and Western Railroad.
- Pass the brown bridge with silver rails of Route 320. (Downstream, right is sloped gravel launch site #5 with a 10-yard carry to a parking lot behind BSB Bank and Trust.)
- Just after the bridge, on your left will be a green metal structure overhanging the water.

- Pass under two more railroad bridges (not as close together this time).
- The next bridge signals the take-out point. Head downstream, right of the brown, silver-railed Route 23 highway bridge.

Date visited:

Notes:

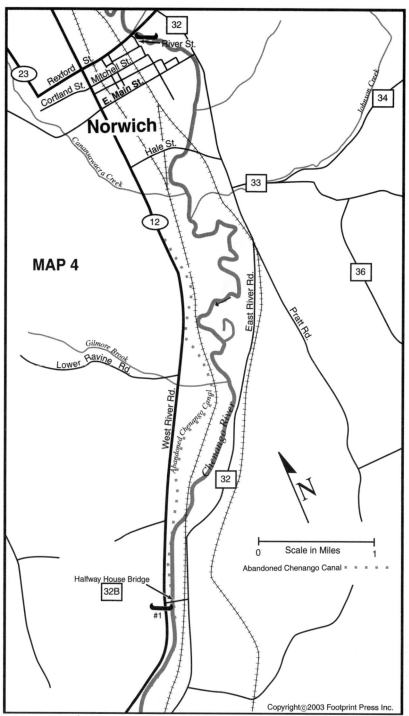

Chenango River (start at Halfway House Road)

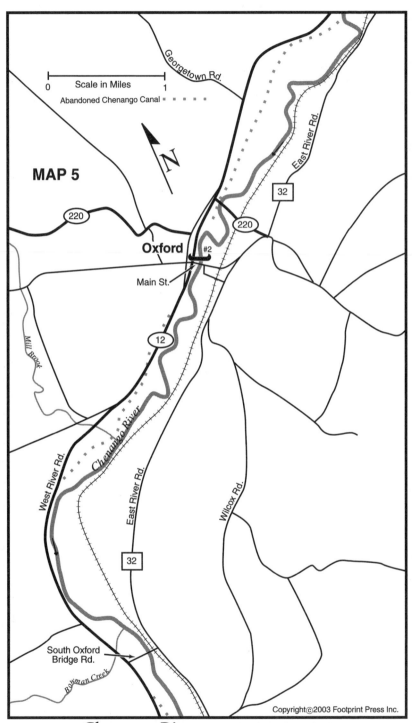

Chenango River (middle through Oxford)

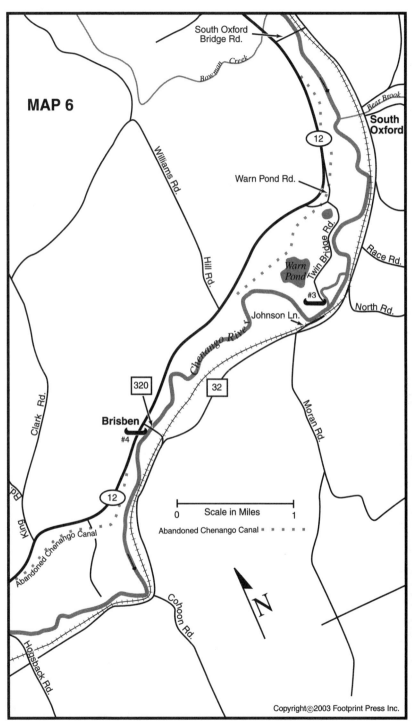

Chenango River (middle through Brisben)

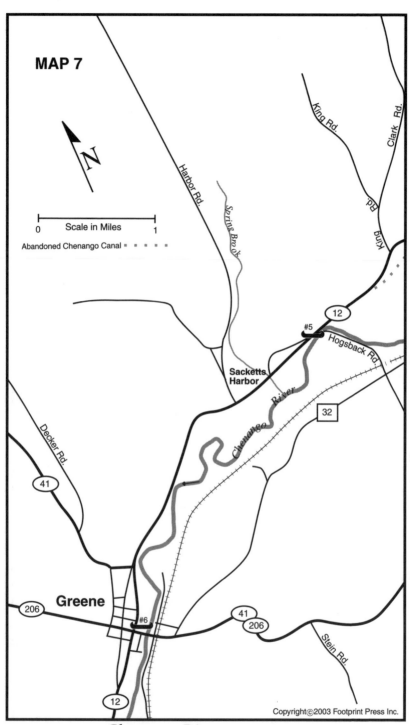

MAP 7

N

Scale in Miles
0   1

Abandoned Chenango Canal ▪ ▪ ▪ ▪ ▪ ▪

King Rd

Clark Rd.

Harbor Rd.

Spring Brook

King Rd.

12

#5

Hogsback Rd.

Sacketts Harbor

Chenango River

32

Decker Rd.

41

206

Greene

#6

41

206

Stein Rd.

12

Copyright©2003 Footprint Press Inc.

Chenango River (end at Greene)

43

CHENANGO RIVER
(South of Norwich to Greene, maps #4 - 7)

Location: Norwich, Oxford, Brisben and Greene, Chenango County (See overall map on page 159 and locator map on page 160.)

Directions: From Norwich, head south on Route 12. Pass Hale Street, then turn left on County Route 32B (Halfway House Road). Immediately on the right is a DEC launch site labeled "Chenango River Boat Access Site."

Launch Site #1: The DEC launch site on Halfway House Road has parking for 6 cars and 3 steps down to a mud shore, downstream, right of the bridge.

Launch Site #2: Continue south on Route 12 into Oxford. Turn left (east) into the parking area at the red NBT Bank sign after Quickway. You're parking behind The Whistling Swan in a small park beside the river with benches and paved walkways. Launch from the rocks below the Main Street bridge.

Launch Site #3: From Route 12, turn east onto Warn Pond Road, then left onto Twin Bridge Road. Continue to the end (one mile from Route 12). A short trail leads to a muddy slope upstream, right of stone bridge abutments.

Launch Site #4: From Route 12 in Brisben near the junction of County Route 320, a DEC sign "Chenango River Angler Parking Area" marks the 4-car parking area and gradual slope to the river downstream, right of the County Route 320 bridge.

Launch Site #5: From Route 12 turn east onto Hogsback Road, north of Sacketts Harbor. Cross over the one-lane rusted, arched bridge to a pull-off area for 6 cars on the left. A short, steep bank leads to a mud and grass sloped water access 50 yards upstream of the bridge.

Take-out Site #6: In Greene turn onto Route 41 south / Route 206 east. Turn left onto the unmarked, paved drive of Rotary Park, just before the bridge. Launch from the right at the short bank, near the dry-hydrant. Park in the parking area at the end of the drive, not near the dry-hydrant.

Best Season to Visit: Spring (except flood stage), summer and fall

Paddling Distance: Total: 21.9 miles

Halfway House bridge to Oxford: 4.2 miles (1.5 hours)

Oxford to Warn Pond Road: 7.6 miles (2.5 hours)

Warn Pond Road to Brisben: 2.6 miles (0.75 hour)

Brisben to Hogsback Road: 3.3 miles (1 hour)

Hogsback Road to Greene: 4.2 miles (1.5 hours)

Estimated Time to Paddle: 6 - 8 hours

Difficulty: (riffles, 6 feet-per-mile gradient from Norwich to Oxford)

(2 feet-per-mile gradient from Oxford to Greene)

Water Level Information: http://waterdata.usgs.gov/ny/nwis/rt (the gage, #01507000, is at Greene, the end of this segment)

Other Activities: Fish, bird watch

Amenities: Norwich, Oxford and Greene have restaurants

Dogs: OK

Admission: Free

Contact: A comprehensive "Chenango River Canoe Guide" can be purchased from Rogers Environmental Education Center (PO Box 716, Sherburne, NY 13460-0716, phone (607) 674-4017) for $2 plus postage.

See page 163 for the section of the Chenango River north of here using maps #1 through #3. It's a faster flowing segment.

By the time the water reaches Norwich it is a wider and slower stream. This section is very scenic with forests shading the waterway and an abundance of plant and animal life. You'll find mostly quiet water with a few riffles interspersed. In low water conditions you may need to drag your boat through some spots.

You can certainly continue south from Greene, but you'll encounter a series of riffles near Chenango Forks with the largest riffles where the Tioughnioga River comes in on the right. There is also a low dam in Binghamton and the scenery is urban.

Paddling Directions:

- Head downstream from the Halfway House Road bridge.
- For a while Route 12 is near the river, then you cross the valley to hug a hill and escape the highway.
- Watch for downed trees on some of the sharp bends or oxbows.
- Pass under the brown Route 220 highway bridge. (No access.)

- Pass under the Main Street bridge in Oxford. (Access (#2) is the rocks under the bridge, right.)
- Mill Brook enters from the right.
- Bowman Creek enters from the right.
- Pass under the South Oxford bridge. (No access.)
- Bear Brook enters from the left.
- The river splits around a big island. Bear left if you want to access the Warn Pond Road bridge and launch site (#3).
- Pass under the brown Brisben Road highway bridge. (Access (#4) is downstream, right.)
- Pass under the Hogsback Road bridge. (Access (#5) is 50 yards upstream, left of the bridge.)
- Spring Brook enters from the right.
- Take-out (#6) is at Rotary Park upstream, right of the Route 206 bridge at a dry-hydrant in Greene.

Date visited:

Notes:

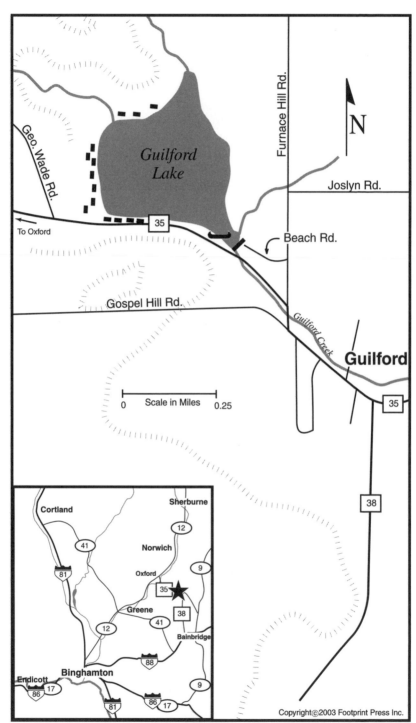

Guilford Lake

44

GUILFORD LAKE

Location: Town of Guilford, Chenango County

Directions: From Route 12, in Oxford, turn south on County Road 35. County Road 35 will head south then east before reaching Guilford Lake. The parking area will be on the left, at the east end of the lake, marked by a brown DEC sign "Guilford Lake Fishing Access."

Launch & Take-out Site: From the parking area you'll find a sloped grassy ramp leading 25 yards to water's edge for hand launching only.

Best Season to Visit: Spring, summer and fall

Paddling Distance: 1.5 miles around the lake

Estimated Time to Paddle: 1 - 2 hours

Difficulty:

Other Activities: Fish

Amenities: None

Dogs: OK

Admission: Free

Contact: DEC, Region 7
615 Erie Boulevard West, Syracuse, NY 13204-2400
(315) 426-7403

Guilford Lake feeds Guilford Creek, which flows through the village of Guilford. Over the years it has changed names from Cable Pond to Guilford Pond to Guilford Lake.

This is a small, deep, peaceful lake, covering 70 acres. It's popular with fishermen who come for the large-mouth bass, panfish, walleyes, chain pickerel and rainbow trout.

At the southeast corner just past the parking area is a dam. North of that are a grassy sidehill and then a wooded shoreline. The far west side of the pond has cottages. Swimming is not allowed near the launch site but looks inviting elsewhere in the pond.

Date visited:

Notes:

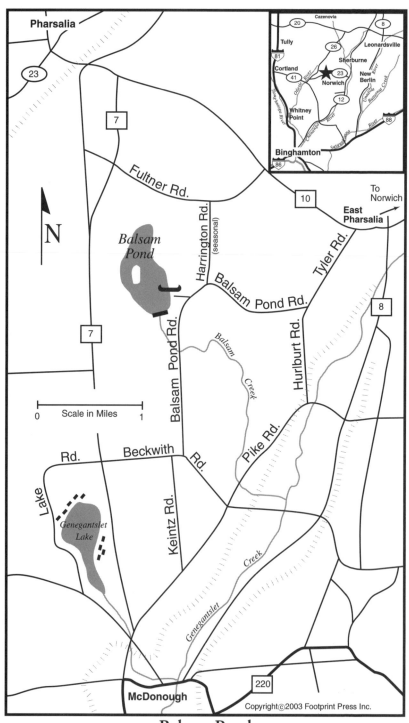

Balsam Pond

45

BALSAM POND

Location:	Town of McDonough, Chenango County
Directions:	From Norwich, head west on County Road 10 passing through Preston and East Pharsalia (pass County Road 8). Take the next left (S) onto Tyler Road (there is no sign at this junction). Take the first right onto Balsam Pond Road. Pass seasonal Harrington Road and take the next right toward Balsam Pond, marked by a brown DEC sign "Balsam Pond Fishing Access."

Launch & Take-out Site: You can park near water's edge, where there's a flat gravel area for hand launching only.

Best Season to Visit: Spring, summer and fall

Paddling Distance: Balsam Pond is approximately 0.9 mile long

Estimated Time to Paddle: 1 to 2 hours

Difficulty: ▸━━◖

Other Activities: Fish, camp

Amenities: Outhouse

Dogs: OK

Admission: Free

Contact: DEC, Region 7
615 Erie Blvd. West, Syracuse, NY 13204-2400
(315) 426-7403

The drive in to this remote, pristine lake was part of the fun. Go slowly and keep a watch for animals. We saw coyote, a large flock of turkeys and a pheasant. Then we arrived at the pond and found primitive camping sites nestled in the woods along the access road. Not a cottage in sight! The south end has a grass-covered dike. The rest of the shoreline is forested, with a tree stump marsh on the east side. There's even a small island to paddle around.

Enjoy the sounds of nature on this 149-acre pond. If fishing's your thing, you'll find rainbow trout and small mouth bass. We'd love to go back in fall when the leaves would be ablaze and we'd have the area to ourselves.

Wooden stumps remain where trees once stood in Balsam Pond.

Date visited:

Notes:

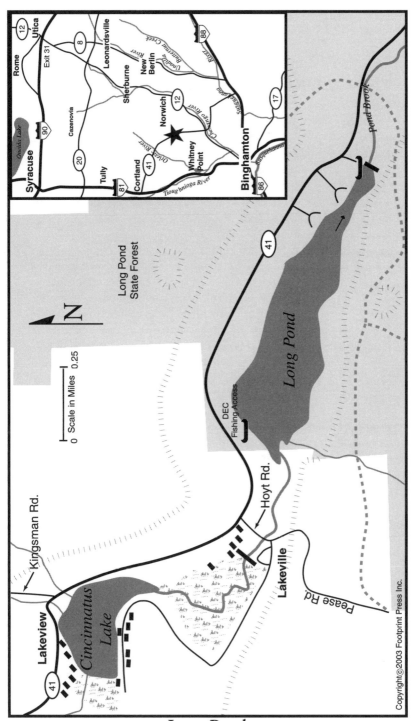

Long Pond

46

LONG POND

Location: Town of Smithville, Chenango County (near the borders of Cortland and Broome Counties)

Directions: From Route 81 in Cortland, take exit 10 and head south on Route 41. Cross the Otselic River and pass Cincinnatus Lake. Watch for the DEC sign marking the parking area on the right (S) side of Route 41 on Long Pond.

Launch & Take-out Site #1: Parking for 10 cars, an almost flat cement ramp, a small metal dock, a 10-yard carry to the water.

Launch & Take-out Site Site #2: You can launch near the earthen dam at the eastern end of the lake. A dirt drive leads to a day-use area with picnic tables and a pedestrian bridge over the outlet. The launch is via an easy grass bank.

Best Season to Visit: Spring and summer (hunting is allowed in fall)

Nearby Campgrounds: A series of dirt roads at the northeast end of Long Pond lead to 10 primitive campsites that are free and available on a first-come basis. Camping for more than three nights or in a group of ten or more requires a permit from a DEC Forest Ranger.

Paddling Distance: Long Pond is one mile long

Estimated Time to Paddle: 1-2 hours

Difficulty: ▶━━◗

Other Activities: Fish, camp, picnic, hike (4 miles of trails are identified by horse trail signs and numbers)

Amenities: Outhouses in the camping areas

Dogs: OK

Admission: Free

Contact: DEC, Region 7
2715 State Highway 80, Sherburne, NY 13460
(607) 674-4036

3,254-acre Long Pond State Forest offers a wide variety of habitats and recreational opportunities, including paddling on Long Pond. Wide swaths of the pond are lily covered. The pond remains undeveloped and tree-lined. Ten secluded campsites dot the northeast end. What a great place to camp for a while and spend your days exploring every inch of the pond and state forest. Each campsite has a fireplace, parking pad and access to a community outhouse. A day use area, with parking and picnic tables is located adjacent to the dam. Follow the snowmobile trail to explore the ruins of the Tarbell homestead during your visit.

Over a thousand acres of land were purchased in the 1930s to create Long Pond State Forest. Old farm fields were reforested to white pine and spruce. Native species of American beech, black cherry, white ash, sugar and red maple and eastern hemlock also can be found. An additional 2,200 acres was purchased in 1963 from the Tarbell estate.

The Tarbell family ownership dated back to 1875, when Eli Tarbell purchased 500 acres around Long Pond. A water-driven sawmill and dam were erected on the Pond to harvest hemlock from the surrounding forest. In 1903, the Tarbells began purchasing dairy cows. During the 1940s and 1950s, the farm flourished as a model of efficiency. The farm employed 35 people, maintained 445 purebred Guernsey cows and bottled 2,800 quarts of milk daily. The "Golden Guernsey" milk was shipped by rail to many of New York City's finest restaurants.

Within Long Pond State Forest, you'll find over 400 acres of grass and brush land. These areas contain breeding populations of two species of sparrows listed as species of special concern because their natural habitat is shrinking statewide. The Henslow sparrow and grasshopper sparrow both require large areas of grassland to survive. Management efforts continue to perpetuate this habitat. The bluebird, New York's official state bird, is also listed as a species of special concern because of habitat loss. Look for the over two dozen strategically placed bluebird houses. These houses have attracted several nesting pairs.

A mature hardwood-hemlock forest is located south of Long Pond. This area, interspersed with wetlands, constitutes an area over 300 acres excluded from timber harvesting. It contains large specimens of hemlock, some over 125 years old. Within this area, the threatened red-shouldered hawk nests. The birds utilize the wetlands when hunting for food and the mature hardwood forest for nesting. The hawk migrates back to the forest in early April, and can be seen soaring over Long Pond.

117-acre Long Pond also offers year-round fishing opportunities. A former state record tiger musky was caught in the pond in 1983. Pond Brook is a trout stream that courses through the forest.

Date visited:

Notes:

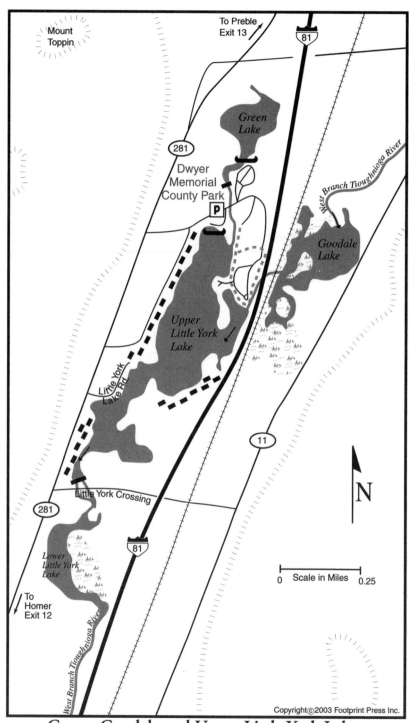

Green, Goodale and Upper Little York Lakes

47

GREEN, GOODALE &
UPPER LITTLE YORK LAKES

Location: Town of Preble, Cortland County

Directions: Take Exit 13 (Preble) off Route 81 and head south on Route 281. In about 3 miles you'll see a sign on the left for Dwyer Memorial County Park. Turn left and follow the road into the park. Continue past the large parking area and large building (home of the Cortland Repertory Theatre). Take the next right (before Green Lake Outlet) to the launch at Upper Little York Lake. For access to Green Lake, take the first left and drive to the back of the loop to the water's edge.

Launch & Take-out Site #1: The official launch site at the north end of Upper Little York Lake has a wide gradually sloped gravel area and a small dock. Launch your boat, then park your vehicle up the hill.

Launch & Take-out Site #2: Shoreline access to Green Lake is via a small grassy bank at the edge of the park road.

Best Season to Visit: Spring and summer (Caution: In October the water level in Goodale Lake is lowered making the upstream paddle from Upper Little York Lake into Goodale Lake difficult due to a strong current.)

Paddling Distance: Upper Little York Lake is 1.2 miles long

Green Lake is 0.5 mile long

From the northern launch on Upper Little York Lake, through Goodale Lake to the mouth of West Branch Tioughnioga River is 1.1 miles.

Goodale Lake is 0.5 miles long

Estimated Time to Paddle: 0.5 hour in Green Lake

2 - 4 hours in Upper Little York and Goodale Lakes

Difficulty: ▮━━━◖

Other Activities: Fishing, hiking trails, picnic areas, playground, wading pool (camping is not allowed)

Amenities: Restrooms, snack bar/restaurant, Cortland Repertory Theatre

Dogs: OK

Admission: Free

Contact: DEC, Region 7
        615 Erie Blvd. West, Syracuse, NY 13204-2400
        (315) 426-7403

        Cortland County Waterfront Development Commission
        Cortland County Business BDC/IDA
        PO Box 549, 26 North Main St., Cortland, NY 13045
        (607) 756-5005

All public access to these lakes is through Dwyer Memorial County Park on the north end of Upper Little York Lake. It is an active day-use park with many amenities for family outings and is home of the Cortland Repertory Theatre, which puts on professional summer stock from June through August.

Green Lake and Goodale Lake each feed south into 2-mile-long Upper Little York Lake, then to Lower Little York Lake. They're all part of the headwaters of the Tioughnioga River and sport crystal clear water. You can easily watch the fish swim below your boat. Green Lake has a few cottages on the western shore and is woodland for the rest of the shoreline. A dam and shallow waterway (not canoeable) connects it with Upper Little York Lake. You can paddle upstream from Upper Little York Lake to Goodale Lake.

The Tioughnioga River Trail project was granted $1 million funding in September 2002 to provide waterfront access for kayaking, canoeing, hiking and biking from Dwyer Memorial Park south to Marathon. Watch for improved access in the years to come.

Green Lake Paddling Directions:
- From the launch, paddle any direction on this small (approximately 0.5 mile long) but picturesque lake. You can't paddle south into Upper Little York Lake.

Upper Little York and Goodale Lakes Paddling Directions:
- From the launch at the north end of Upper Little York Lake, paddle toward the left heading southeast. (If you paddle south, it's approximately 1.2 miles to the dams at Little York Crossing.)
- Continue south along the shore then head north as you round a small peninsula.
- Paddle north through Goodale Lake Outlet, passing under I-81 and railroad bridges. (It's approximately 0.6 mile from here to the start of West Branch Tioughnioga River).
- Explore the small islands and jagged shore of uninhabited Goodale Lake.

- Return south out the outlet to Upper Little York Lake, then paddle south on the lake.
- The twin dams at the south end of the lake is as far as you can go. Return to the launch at the north end.

Date visited:

Notes:

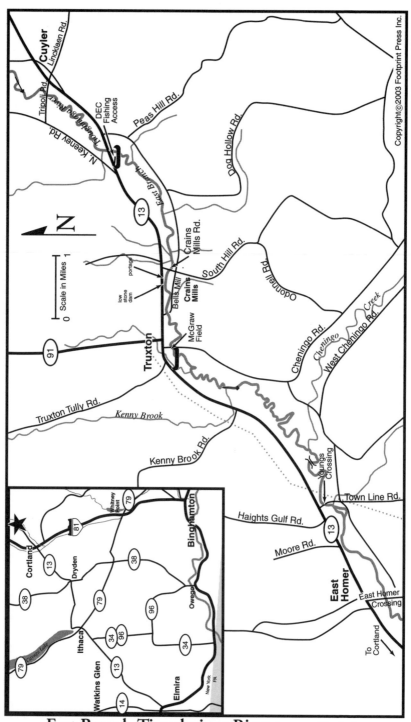

East Branch Tioughnioga River (start at Cuyler)

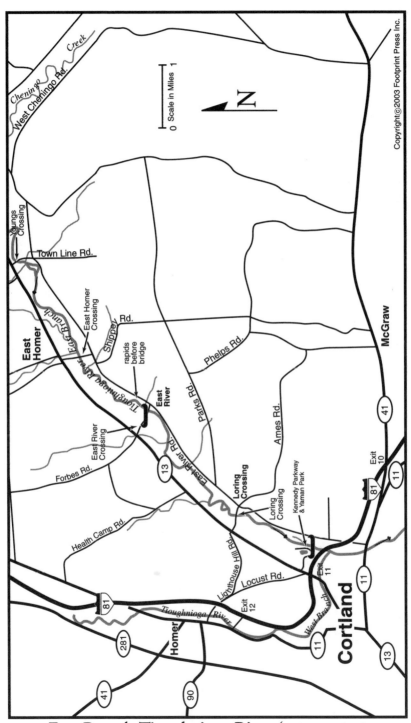

East Branch Tioughnioga River (end at Cortland)

48

EAST BRANCH TIOUGHNIOGA RIVER
(Cuyler to Cortland)

Location: Cuyler, Truxton, East Homer and Corning, Cortland County

Directions: From Cortland, follow Route 13 north through Truxton. After North Keeney Road, watch to the right for the DEC Fishing Access Site.

Launch Site #1: South of Cuyler on Route 13 is a DEC Fishing Access Site. Overnight parking is not allowed. River access is via a grassy bank.

Launch Site #2: From Route 13 in Truxton head south on Cheningo Road to cross the East Branch Tioughnioga River. Shortly on the right will be McGraw Field, a baseball field with access to a bank on the river, downstream, right. (McGraw Field is named after John McGraw the acclaimed field manager of the New York Giants in the early 1900s. McGraw was born in Truxton.)

Launch Site #3: Park along the road at East River Crossing. Water access is upstream or downstream, right.

Take-out Site: At Yaman Park in Cortland. From Route 13, just north of the Route 81 overpass in Cortland, turn right (E) onto Kennedy Parkway. Enter Yaman Park and drive to the back, around the right side of the pond. River access is down a small grassy bank.

Best Season to Visit: Spring: put in at Cuyler
Fall or summer: put in at Truxton

Nearby Campgrounds: Forest Lake Campground, 6019 Dog Hollow Road, Cuyler, (607) 842-6401
Country Music Park Campground, 1804 Route 13, Cortland, (607) 753-0377
Yellow Lantern Kampground, 1770 Route 13 North Cortland, 13045, (607) 756-2959

Paddling Distance: Total: 19.9 miles
Cuyler launch site to Truxton: 4.3 miles
Truxton to East River Crossing: 10.7 miles
East River Crossing to Yaman Park: 4.9 miles

Estimated Time to Paddle: 5-6 hours in spring

Difficulty: (5 feet-per-mile gradient on average, moderate current, riffles)

Water Level Information: http://waterdata.usgs.gov/ny/nwis/rt (the gage, #01509000, is in Cortland at the end of this segment)

Other Activities: Fish, Yaman Park has a swimming pond, picnic facilities, a skateboard park, and a playground

Amenities: Yaman Park has restrooms and showers (Memorial Day through Labor Day, 6 AM - 10:30 PM)

Dogs: Not allowed in Yaman Park

Admission: Free

Contact: Yaman Park, City of Cortland, Recreation 25 Court Street, Cortland NY 13045

The Tioughnioga (pronounced tie-uff-nee-oh-ga) River forms from two main branches—the East and West before reaching the Susquehanna River. The East Branch Tioughnioga River flows through a wide valley. This stream must rip-roar in early spring as evidenced by the massive piles of tree debris at curves.

Between Cuyler and Truxton, several trees are down across the stream. In medium water you can paddle over most, but must portage around one (an easy portage.) There's also a low stone dam which can be paddled through a breech. The whole section has minor riffles and twists and turns but no sharp bends. Junked cars litter the shores in several places.

In low water conditions or to avoid these obstacles, put in at Truxton. You'll have a clear but winding channel with ripples, but no impediments all the way to Cortland. The one exception is a very small run of rapids just north of East River Crossing.

The river (actually more the size of a creek) winds through woods and wilds. We saw great blue herons and hawks as well as the usual ducks and geese. Civilization doesn't begin to encroach until south of East River Crossing. Because this river flows southwest we did encounter a headwind when paddling on a warm, sunny day in April.

Paddling Directions:
- From the Route 13, DEC fishing access lot below Cuyler, head downstream.
- Shortly, pass over submerged pilings from an old railroad bridge.
- Watch for trees across the channel as it bends wildly.
- Pass the brown metal bridge of Crains Mills Road.
- Portage to the left around a fallen tree that blocks the channel.

- Run through the breech of a low stone dam.
- In Truxton you'll find the blue metal bridge of Cheningo Road. (Continue past the bridge. Downstream, right you'll find a bank to McGraw Field.)
- The river continues its contorted ribbon of bends.
- Pass under an old railroad bridge.
- Pass under overhead power lines.
- At Youngs Crossing the silver bridge is high above water level.
- The East Homer Crossing bridge is silver metal with low sides. (A small ledge is available upstream of the bridge. You can park along East Homer Crossing and launch downstream, left.)
- Run a small set of short, easy rapids.
- At East River Crossing the bridge has a low green superstructure. (You can park along the road with a bank to river access downstream, right.)
- Pass the aged, arched cement Loring Crossing bridge. (There is a one car pull-off and a grassy bank to river access upstream, right.)
- Take-out is upstream, right just before the I-81 bridge (a high green bridge on round cement pillars) and up a grassy bank to Yaman Park.

Date visited:

Notes:

49

GLOVER POND

Location:	Town of Cincinnatus, Cortland County (See the Otselic River map on page 192.)
Directions:	From Route 81 in Cortland take exit 10 and head south on Route 41. After the Route 26 junction, turn right (W) on Gee Brook Road. Turn right on Beach Road and watch for the parking and launch area on the left when you reach Glover Pond.

Launch & Take-out Site: A sloped gravel launch ramp at the parking area.

Best Season to Visit: Spring, summer and fall

Paddling Distance: Glover Pond is 0.3 miles long

Estimated Time to Paddle: 0.5 - 1 hour

Difficulty: ▸━━●

Other Activities: Fish

Amenities: None

Dogs: OK

Admission: Free

Contact: DEC, Region 7
615 Erie Boulevard. West, Syracuse, NY 13204-2400
(315) 426-7403

This body of water has an identity crisis. We've seen it called Glover's Pond (historical records), Papish Pond (by DEC) and High Lake (on a topo map). Glover's Pond derives from a mill John Glover and his son, John H. Glover erected in the mid-1800s.

However, it's pretty no matter what you call it. It's a pristine tree-lined pond nestled below a woodland cliff on the south shore. The northwest end is dotted with lilies and a marsh of old tree stumps.

Date visited:

Notes:

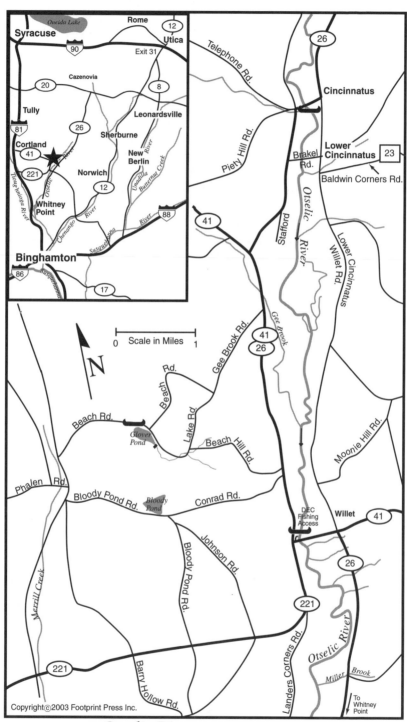

Otselic River (start at Cincinnatus)

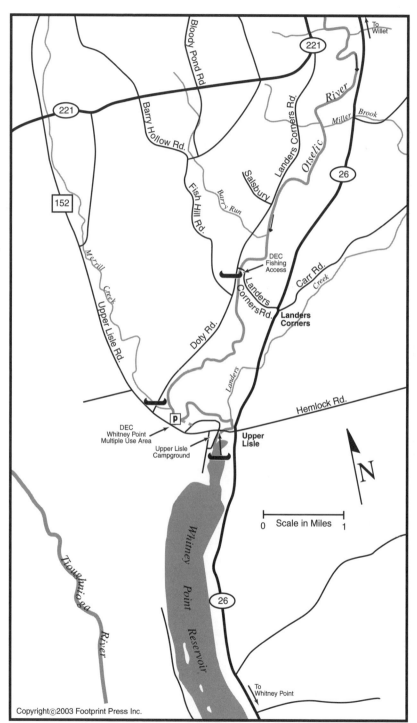

Otselic River (end at Whitney Point Reservoir)

50

OTSELIC RIVER
(Cincinnatus to Whitney Point Reservoir)

Location: Cincinnatus, Willet, Landers Corners, Whitney Point and Upper Lisle, Cortland and Broome Counties

Directions: From I-81 south of Cortland, take either Route 41 southeast or Route 221 east. Then take Route 26 north to Cincinnatus. On the east side of the river is the fire house with a town park next to it.

Launch Site #1: From the town park in Cincinnatus, steps lead down to water level.

Launch Site #2: Off Routes 26/41 west of the river from Willet is a DEC site labeled "Otselic River Fishing Access" with parking for 12 cars and a moderately steep bank to a muddy water's edge.

Launch Site #3: A DEC fishing access site off Landers Corners Road on the east side of the creek, near the bridge has a 6-car lot and a moderately steep grass slope to water level.

Take-out Site: In Upper Lisle Campground on the north end of Whitney Point Reservoir. From Route 26 turn west on Upper Lisle Road (Broome County Route 152). There is a yellow sign for "Knickerbockers" on the corner. Take a left immediately after the Otselic River bridge. You'll find a slightly sloped gravel launch, a Porta-potty and picnic tables.

Best Season to Visit: Spring (in other seasons launch from Willet)

Nearby Campgrounds: Upper Lisle Campground, Route 26, Upper Lisle (607) 692-4612

Paddling Distance: Total: 14.3 miles
 Cincinnatus launch to Willet: 5.1 miles
 Willet to Landers Corners Road: 5.4 miles
 Landers Corners Road to Upper Lisle: 3.8 miles

Estimated Time to Paddle: 4 hours in Spring

Difficulty: (small riffles, mild current, 4 to 8 feet-per-mile gradient)

Water Level Information: http://waterdata.usgs.gov/ny/nwis/rt (the gage in Cincinnatus at the start of this segment, #01510000)

Other Activities:	Fish, hike in Upper Lisle Campground
Amenities:	Restaurant near bridge in Cincinnatus
	Porta-potty and picnic table at take-out
Dogs:	OK
Admission:	Free

Otselic is an Indian word for "wild plumbs." See if you can spot any along the shores as you paddle this scenic waterway. Upstream from Cincinnatus it's shallow, rock strewn and sinister. The way is blocked by nasty strainers and frequent barbed wire. So, head downstream (of course). You'll find a remote, wilderness stream where the predominate sounds are made by birds. Wildlife is abundant. We spotted mink, deer, turtles, muskrats, hawks, geese, ducks and songbirds. The stream cuts a swath through sand banks with lots of twists and turns around islands but no sharp turns. Below Willet the water is deeper and slower, making it an easy moving water paddle.

The take-out point is the northern end of the Whitney Point Reservoir. This is a long lake formed by a mile-wide dam at its southern end. It was built between 1938 and 1942 as a flood control measure after major floods overwhelmed the Chenango River basin in 1934 and 1935. In summer the reservoir is 4 miles long, in winter it can be 3.5 miles long as the water level is lowered. Because of this variable lake level, the conditions you find at the end of this paddling route could vary. You can certainly paddle in Whitney Point Reservoir but, like any large lake, wind can be a factor.

Paddling Directions:
- Head downstream from the Cincinnatus bridge.
- In 0.75 mile pass under a green bridge. (Downstream, right a 25-yard carry leads to a parking area off Brakel Road, Lower Cincinnatus.)
- The river heads due south, hugging a steep hill on the right.
- Proceed through a long, winding stretch with islands to paddle around. In low water you may have to push through shallow areas.
- At 5.5 miles, pass under a high bridge that's green with silver rails. (Upstream, right is a DEC parking area labeled "Otselic River Fishing Access" off Routes 26/41, near the corner of Route 221 in Willet.)
- The waterway straightens out a bit and the water is generally deeper.
- At 11 miles, pass under the arched green metal bridge of Landers Corners Road. (Downstream left is easy access to a DEC parking area labeled "Landers Corners Fishing Access.")

- Merrill Creek will merge from the right. (Up the creek is a small 2-car parking area and launch off Doty Road.)
- At the next sharp bend, on your right and up a small bank is the DEC parking area labeled "Whitney Point Multiple Use Area." It's hard to see from water level.
- Continue to wind around big bends through a mud flats area. If the reservoir is full, the water will deepen and you'll loose current. You may encounter wind as you round the bend at the top of the reservoir.
- Pass under a low, brown metal bridge to the northern end of Whitney Point Reservoir. Immediately turn right downstream of the bridge to find the take-out at Upper Lisle Campground.

Date visited:

Notes:

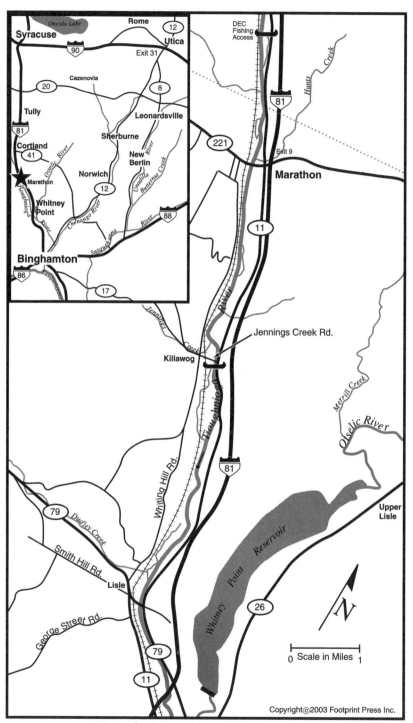

Tioughnioga River (start at Marathon)

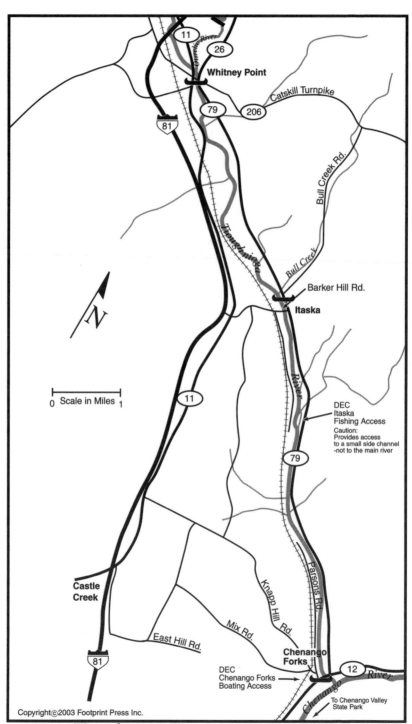

Tioughnioga River (end at Chenango Forks)

51

TIOUGHNIOGA RIVER
(Marathon to Chenango Forks)

Location: Marathon, Killawog, Lisle, Whitney Point, Itaska and Chenango Forks, Broome County

Directions: Take exit 9 (Marathon) from I-81 and head north on Route 11. 1.2 miles north of the main intersection in Marathon is a DEC fishing access site on the left side, across from an American Legion building (Osco Robinson Post #617). It's marked by a brown DEC sign "Tioughnioga River Public Fishing Stream."

Launch Site #1: From the DEC access site on Route 11, north of Marathon, there is a short bank down to river level.

Launch Site #2: From the Jennings Creek Road bridge, upstream, right.

Launch Site #3: Heading north into Whitney Point on Route 11 there's a small road to the right immediately before the Route 206 intersection that leads to water access below the Route 206 bridge. There's a gravel shore and room for several cars under the green arched bridge.

Launch Site #4: In Itaska you can access the water from the Barker Hill Road bridge, downstream, right, or, from a pull-off area just north of Itaska on Route 79 that leads to a grass bank used by fishermen.

Take-out Site: On the south side of the Route 12 bridge over the Tioughnioga River in Chenango Forks is a 6-car parking lot marked by a brown DEC sign "Chenango Forks Boat Access Site."

Best Season to Visit: Spring, summer and fall

Nearby Campgrounds: Chenango Valley State Park
153 State Park Road, Chenango Forks, NY 13746
(607) 648-5251

Paddling Distance: Total: 20.9 miles
Marathon launch to Jennings Creek Road: 4.5 miles
Jennings Creek Road to Whitney Point: 6.5 miles
Whitney Point to Itaska: 4.2 miles
Itaska to Chenango Forks: 5.7 miles

Estimated Time to Paddle: 4 - 5 hours in Spring

Difficulty: (average 7 feet-per-mile gradient, a great moving water run for novices)

Water Level Information: http://waterdata.usgs.gov/ny/nwis/rt (the gage, #001512500, is on the Chenango River at Chenango Forks, downstream from this segment)

Other Activities: Fish

Amenities: Aiello's Ristorante and a Hess mini-mart are near the Route 206 bridge in Whitney Point.

Dogs: OK

Admission: Free

Canoeing on the Tioughnioga River.

The Tioughnioga (pronounced tie-uff-nee-oh-ga) River basin was used extensively by Native Americans for fishing and hunting. They named it "river with bank of flowers," which is a hint of the beauty that awaits the paddler.

Looking at the map may turn you away from this waterway. It does parallel many roadways and highways and you're never out of eyesight or earshot of civilization. Still, this is a very pleasant river to paddle and we recommend you give it a try. The river flows in a wide valley with low banks providing a panoramic view rimmed with farm-dotted hills. For a waterway through civilization, there's little trash. The banks are lined in daffodils, ferns, or white trillium, depending on when you paddle. You'll find a gently flowing current in a wide waterway with plenty of islands beckoning you to stop for a break or picnic.

North of Marathon this river is canoeable, but sharp turns, strainers and rapids make it an intermediate to expert stream. More experienced paddlers put in in Homer and paddle through Cortland and Blodgett Mills to Marathon. The section of river described here has been designated a New York State Heritage Waterway and was named the Tioughnioga River Trail. Improvements are slated for the coming years to enhance river access and develop hiking trails.

Paddling Directions:

- From the DEC access site on Route 11, north of Marathon, head downstream.
- Pass through Marathon and under the old, arched green metal Route 221 bridge.
- The Delaware Lackawanna and Western Railroad tracks will be near the right bank.
- At Killawog, pass under the arched green Jennings Creek Road bridge. (Access is upstream, right.)
- At Lisle pass under the brown Route 79 highway bridge.
- Pass under the double bridges of I-81.
- In Whitney Point pass under Route 11, a green highway bridge with green rails.
- Just after the bridge, the Otselic River (outflow from the Whitney Point Reservoir) will merge from the left.
- Quickly, pass under a green, double arched bridge (Route 206). You're still in Whitney Point. (Access is under the bridge, right. A small road leads up to Route 11.)
- At a bend in the river, just before the bridge with big brown metal arches in Itaska, is a grass landing on the left with access to a pull-off area along Route 79 that is used by fishermen.
- Pass the Itaska bridge. (Access is possible downstream, right through brush.)
- Head to the right bank as you approach the Route 12 bridge (a brown highway bridge with silver rails) in Chenango Forks. A gravel bank under the bridge makes a nice take-out with a 50-yard carry to the DEC parking lot. If you go under a railroad bridge, you've gone too far.

Note: You can continue to paddle beyond these bridges and head downstream (S) on the Chenango River, but expect to find whirlpools, debris and sandbars at the confluence and a fast run on the Chenango River. It is not recommended for beginners. A possible take-out point is the left bank at Chenango Valley State Park, but it is tricky to locate and rangers discourage take-out here unless you have a camping permit.

Date visited:

Notes:

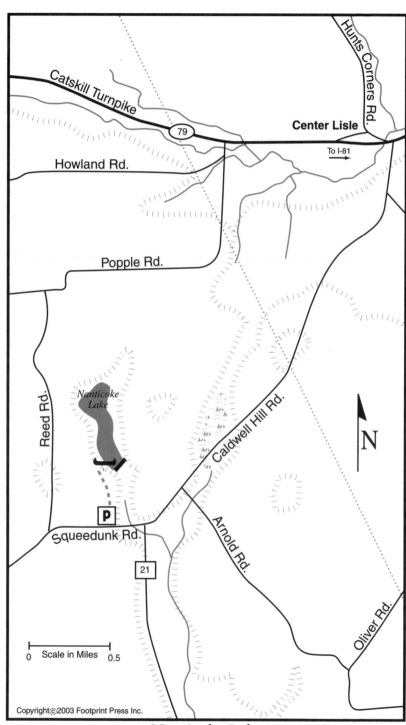

Nanticoke Lake

52

NANTICOKE LAKE

Location: Town of Lisle, Broome County
Directions: Exit Route 81 at Whitney Point. In Whitney Point
                        take Route 79 west (it's also Route 11 North at this
                        point). Continue west on Route 79 through Lisle and
                        Manningville. Turn left (S) on Caldwell Hill Road in
                        Center Lisle. Bear right as the road becomes Squeedunk
                        Road and watch for the brown DEC sign "Nanticoke
                        Lake Fishing Access" on the right.
Launch & Take-out Site: From the parking area you have to hand carry
                        your boat for 500 yards along a grassy lane. The lake is
                        up a hill and out of sight. At the lake, there's a nice
                        sand and gravel shore for launching.
Best Season to Visit: Spring and summer
Paddling Distance: Nanticoke Lake is approximately 0.7 mile long
Estimated Time to Paddle: 0.5 - 1 hour
Difficulty: (a long carry)
Other Activities: Fish, hunt
Amenities: None
Dogs: OK
Admission: Free
Contact: DEC, Region 7
                        615 Erie Blvd. West, Syracuse, NY 13204-2400
                        (315) 426-7403

The long carry to the water's edge means this will be your own private lake. The lake is formed by an earthen berm at the south end and tree-lined shores elsewhere. You're away from roads and all remnants of civilization so enjoy the sounds and sights of nature.

DEC stocks this lake with rainbow trout. Hunting is allowed on the lands around the lake, so you may want to avoid paddling here in fall.

Paddling Directions:
   • Explore at will.

Nanticoke Lake to yourself - ah, sweet serenity.

Date visited:

Notes:

Paddles in Steuben, Schuyler, Chemung, Tompkins and Tioga Counties

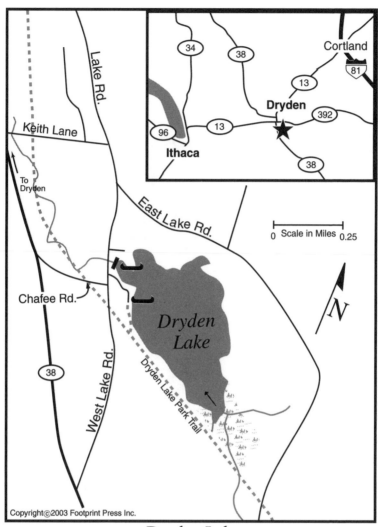

Copyright©2003 Footprint Press Inc.

Dryden Lake

53

DRYDEN LAKE

Location: Dryden, Tompkins County

Directions: From Ithaca, follow Route 13 east to Dryden. In Dryden take Route 38 south. Turn left (E) onto Keith Lane, then right (S) on Lake Road. The two parking areas for Dryden Lake Park will be on the left near the outlet creek.

Launch & Take-out Site #1: The parking area north of the dam has room for 10 cars and a sloped asphalt ramp.

Launch & Take-out Site #2: The parking area south of the dam has a short trail to a sloped dirt launch.

Best Season to Visit: Spring, summer and fall

Paddling Distance: Dryden Lake is 0.8 mile long

Estimated Time to Paddle: About 2 hours to paddle the circumference

Difficulty: ▶━━◼

Other Activities: Fish, hike, bike, bird watch, playground (no swimming)

Amenities: Picnic tables, restrooms near parking areas

Dogs: OK on leash

Admission: Free (dawn to dusk)

Contact: Town of Dryden
65 East Main Street, Dryden, NY 13053
(607) 844-8619
www.dryden.ny.us

120-acre Dryden Lake is surrounded by Dryden Lake Park, replete with picnic areas, pavilions, a playground, restrooms, and fishing/observation platforms. It also sits at the midpoint of the 4-mile-long Dryden Lake Park Trail, which began its existence as the Southern Central Railroad in 1865. Before that, Indians used this area as a campground and settlers built a sawmill here.

In June, we watched carp jump out of the water in their spawning dance. Later in summer, vegetation mats the lake. The area abounds in geese, herons, ospreys, swallows, etc. Several species of turtles sun themselves on the logs. Beavers can be seen too. Take your time and enjoy the plants and animals as you paddle this picturesque lake that is ringed with forests, a golf course and farmlands.

Dryden Lake beckons you to come explore.

Paddling Directions:
- Paddle in either direction around this lake.
- At the south end is a marsh and the inlet creek that is blocked by a large beaver dam.

Date visited:

Notes:

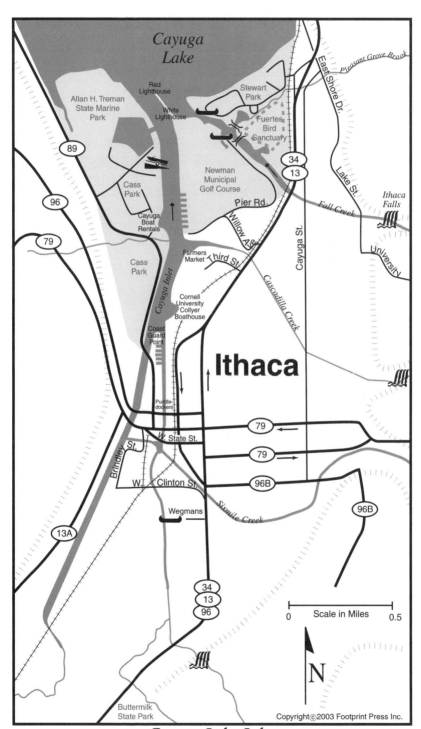

Cayuga Lake Inlet

54

CAYUGA LAKE INLET

Location: Ithaca, Tompkins County

Directions: From Route 13/34 in Ithaca, turn north onto Willow Avenue. Cross the railroad tracks and follow Willow until it ends. Take a right onto Pier Road and circle around the Newman Municipal Golf Course. Turn right at the Ithaca Fire Department training area. Park in the wide dirt area at the end of the road.

Launch Site #1: An easy dirt bank at the end of Pier Road.

Launch Site #2: At a small dock on the park road at the western end of Stewart Park.

Take-out Site: Behind Wegmans on Routes 34/13/96, south of Sixmile Creek.

Best Season to Visit: Spring, summer and fall

Paddling Distance: Total: 4.2 miles
Explore Fall Creek to Cayuga Lake: 2 miles
Up Cayuga Inlet to Wegmans: 2.2 miles

Estimated Time to Paddle: 1 - 2 hours

Difficulty: ▸━━ (You'll encounter strong current upstream in Fall Creek. There can be waves and wind on Cayuga Lake.)

Other Activities: Fish, hike and bird watch in the bird sanctuary

Amenities: Stewart Park has a concession stand, picnic areas, tennis courts, a playground, a restored carousel, athletic fields, a duck pond, a spray pool, a rose garden and trails through a bird sanctuary. (Swimming is not allowed.)

Cayuga Inlet has docks where restaurants and bars serve the water traffic.

Cayuga Boat Rentals, (607) 277-5072, with a dock in Cass Park off Route 89, offers canoe & kayak rentals.

Puddledockers Boat Rental / Charters, 704 ½ N. Buffalo Street, Ithaca, 14850, (607) 273-0096, www.paddledockers.com offers kayak rentals, lessons and tours.

Dogs: OK

Admission: Free
Contact: Stewart Park
NYS Routes 13 and 34, Ithaca, NY 14850
(607) 273-8364

This is a leisurely paddle with much to look at. Along the way, docks offer restaurants, bars and an ice cream shop with outdoor seating, so you may want to plan on a break.

From either launch site you can explore several waterways, including Fall Creek, Pleasant Grove Brook, Cayuga Inlet, Cascadilla Creek, and Sixmile Creek. Admittedly, most of these are loaded with waterfalls upstream so you can't get very far, but you can explore the northern reaches of each. (See the guidebooks *200 Waterfalls in Central & Western New York* for details on exploring the many waterfalls in and near Ithaca.)

Near the start, Stewart Park is an active park with many facilities. Adjacent to the park is the Fuertes Wild Fowl Preserve and Renwick Bird Sanctuary. Named for a former Ithaca Mayor, Stewart Park was formerly Renwick Park, site of the early movie industry in Ithaca (1912-1920). Park buildings date to the time when Pearl White, Lionel Barrymore, and Irene Castle were featured in films made here.

Along the way, you'll pass the Cayuga Inlet Lighthouse. It's a 25-foot-tall tower that was first built in 1917 on the other side of the creek entrance. In 1927, it was moved to its present location at Lighthouse Point. The tower has wood framing and is covered with sheet metal plates. The white light at the top is a solar-powered rotating beacon.

We describe a one-way paddling route, but this area can easily be paddled as a round-trip if you don't want to deal with spotting a car at the take-out.

Paddling Directions:
- From the Pier Road launch site, head upstream on Fall Creek, under a pedestrian bridge. Depending on the water level, you should be able to paddle under a railroad bridge, the Route 13/34 bridge, and the Cayuga Street bridge before it gets too shallow and the current becomes too strong. Turn around and head back downstream.
- Return under the pedestrian bridge and turn right to pass under a second pedestrian bridge. You can paddle a short distance to explore the inlet between Stewart Park and Fuertes Bird Sanctuary.
- Upon leaving the inlet, turn right, downstream into Fall Creek. Continue out to Cayuga Lake and bear left to round the red buoy marker. If the wind and waves are high, you can portage over the peninsula near Lighthouse Point.

- Paddle upstream on Cayuga Inlet. Even in spring, it has no discernable current. Pass a marina and powerboat launch on the right.
- Pass boat slips on the left.
- Pass the Farmer's Market on the left.
- Pass the Cornell University Collyer Boat House on the left.
- Bear left at Coast Guard Point past big yachts under cover on your right. Along the way, docks offer access to restaurants, bars and ice cream shops with outdoor seating.
- Pass under the Route 96 bridge, then the Route 79 bridge.
- The third bridge you pass under is labeled West State Street.
- Continue straight across the Sixmile Creek channel.
- Before railroad tracks, you'll see three 4-foot tubes on the left. Don't worry, you don't have to go through them! Bear right under the railroad trestle.
- Cross under the West Clinton Street bridge.
- Watch for the bank on the left to take-out to the Wegmans parking lot.

Date visited:

Notes:

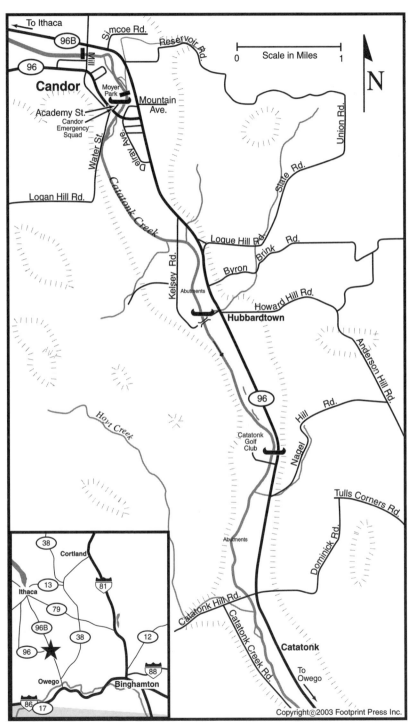

Catatonk Creek (start at Candor)

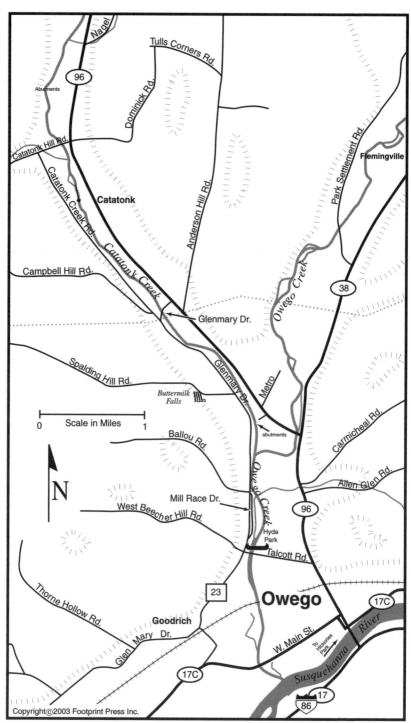

Catatonk Creek (end at Owego)

55

CATATONK CREEK
(Candor to Owego)

Location: Candor, Catatonk and Owego, Tioga County

Directions: Take Route 96B south from Ithaca to Candor. Or, from Owego, take Route 38 north, then Route 96 north to Candor. In Candor, turn west on Route 96, cross Catatonk Creek and turn right onto Academy Street. Park on the right at Moyer Park.

Launch Site #1:   In Moyer Park cross the grass for 150 feet to launch from a gravel bank below the dam.

Launch Site #2:   A pull-off area (unlabeled) slightly north of the road to Catatonk Golf Club on Route 96 provides access to a sloped grass launch.

Take-out Site: The back entrance to Hyde Park is off Talcott Road, immediately east of the Catatonk Creek bridge. There is no sign, just pull in and park at the end toward the bridge. A sloped grass ramp leads to water level below the bridge.

Best Season to Visit: Spring

Nearby Campgrounds: Hickories Park, Town of Owego, Route 17C, Owego, NY 13827, (607) 687-1199

Paddling Distance: Total: 10.1 miles

Candor to Route 96 near Golf Course: 4.0 miles

Route 96 near Golf Course to Glenmary Drive: 3.4 miles

Glenmary Drive to Talcott Road: 2.7 miles

Additional: Talcott Road to Susquehanna River: 1.4 miles, plus 4.2 miles more to Hickories Park

Estimated Time to Paddle: 4 hours in spring

Difficulty: (small riffles, 7 feet-per-mile gradient, no sharp turns)

Water Level Information: http://waterdata.usgs.gov/ny/nwis/route (the gage, #01513831, is in the Susquehanna River in Owego, the extension to this trip)

Other Activities: Fish

Amenities: Moyer Park has a playground and picnic pavilion. Hyde Park has little league fields, restrooms, a picnic pavilion and a soda machine.

Dogs:	OK
Admission:	Free
Contact:	DEC, Region 7
	1285 Fisher Avenue, Cortland, NY 13045
	(607) 753-3095

Catatonk Creek begins in Spencer Lake and travels south to Spencer, east to Candor, then southeast until it joins the Owego Creek just north of Owego. It is navigable from Spencer to Candor, but we don't recommend this section. Paddling is impeded by low bridges, dams, low water and barbed wire fences crossing the waterway. The segment from Candor to Owego, however, is very pleasant and is suitable for beginners. You'll encounter shallow sections early on as the stream splits around islands. Then it becomes a deeper, fairly wide creek with lush, forested banks. The bottom section has some road noise and one place where a log across the stream produces a small drop.

Bring your fishing pole. These waters have largemouth and small-mouth bass and brown trout.

At Owego, Owego Creek meets the Susquehanna River. The take-out point described here is well before the Susquehanna. However, you could extend your trip and continue into the Susquehanna River. Turn left and paddle upstream to Hickories Park or Hiawatha Island as described on page 219. It would be an additional 5.6 miles to Hickories Park on the Susquehanna.

Paddling Directions:
- Head downstream from below the dam in Moyer Park, Candor.
- Pass under the Route 96 bridge and around big islands.
- Pass under the green Kelsey Road bridge.
- Pass old bridge abutments and power lines overhead.
- Pass under a second Kelsey Road bridge. This one is a rusted brown bridge that's closed to traffic. (Water access is upstream, left from the dead-end South Kelsey Road.)
- Within sight of the green bridge with no superstructure, you'll pass a sloped grass access point on the left.
- Then quickly pass under the green bridge. It's the access road to Catatonk Golf Club.
- Pass old bridge abutments.
- Pass under the Catatonk Hill Road bridge, an old rusted highway bridge on cement pillars. (You can park at the go-kart track west of this bridge and carry to a gradual bank downstream, right.)

216

- Pass under the old green highway bridge of Glenmary Drive, then under overhead power lines. (Park along Glenmary Drive for a gradual, sloped grass access downstream, right.)
- Pass old bridge abutments.
- Bear right as you meet Owego Creek to continue downstream. The stream current will increase.
- Take-out is at Hyde Park, upstream, left of the next bridge (Talcott Street) in Owego.

Date visited:

Notes:

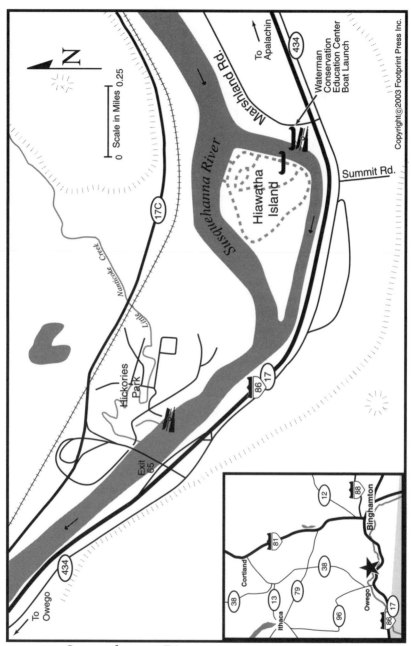

Susquehanna River (around Hiawatha Island)

56

SUSQUEHANNA RIVER
(around Hiawatha Island)

Location: Apalachin, Tioga County

Directions: From I-86 (old Route 17) take exit 65 east of Owego and head east on Route 434. Turn left onto Marshland Road. The second left leads to the Town of Owego boat launch. The third left is to the Waterman Conservation Education Center boat launch.

Launch & Take-out Site #1: The Town of Owego boat launch is marked by a brown sign "Town of Owego Boat Launch." It offers an easy launch via a sloped cement ramp, picnic tables, and a Porta-potty.

Launch & Take-out Site #2: The Waterman Conservation Education Center boat launch is marked by a white sign "Hiawatha Island & River Front Park." It offers an easy launch via a sloped grassy ramp, a small dock, picnic tables, and a Porta-potty.

Launch & Take-out Site #3: To reach Hickories Park boat launch, cross the bridge over the river heading toward Route 17C. Bear left off the bridge and cross Route 17C. The road will bend to parallel the river. Cross under the bridge and over Little Nanticoke Creek. Take the first right to the boat launch, which is a paved slope with nearby parking.

Best Season to Visit: Summer and fall (expect high water and strong currents in spring)

Nearby Campgrounds: Hickories Park, Town of Owego, Route 17C, Owego, NY 13827, (607) 687-1199

Paddling Distance: Around Hiawatha Island is 2.1 miles.
To Hickories Park & back around the island is 3.5 miles.

Estimated Time to Paddle: 1 - 2 hours around Hiawatha Island

Difficulty: ⊱⬛ ⊱⬛

Water Level Information: http://waterdata.usgs.gov/ny/nwis/route (the gage, #01513831, is in the Susquehanna River in Owego, 4.2 miles downstream of this segment.)

Other Activities:	Fish, picnic, hike on Hiawatha Island
Amenities:	Porta-potties at launch sites
	Hickories Park has camping facilities, picnic areas,
	fitness trails, playgrounds, sport fields and restrooms
Dogs:	OK on leash
Admission:	Free
Contact:	Waterman Conservation Education Center
	403 Hilton Road, PO Box 377, Apalachin, NY 13732
	(607) 625-2221
	www.watermancenter.org
	Hickories Park, Town of Owego
	PO Box 248, Owego, NY 13827
	(607) 687-1199

The Susquehanna River between Owego and Apalachin is wide and slow. From the boat launches off Marshland Road you can circle Hiawatha Island or extend your paddle with a trip downstream to Hickories Park. On your way, toss a line overboard and join the many people angling for walleye, bass and tiger muskellunge.

The Waterman Conservation Education Center is dedicated to increasing environmental awareness and outdoor recreation. Waterman operates four wildlife refuges, one of which is 112-acre Hiawatha Island, the largest island in the Susquehanna River within New York State. It's named after the Iroquois warrior who met here for Indian councils. The island is within the 100-year flood plain, and yet for most of the year it is above water. It provides a diverse mix of wet woods, open fields, overgrown meadows, forests and 2 miles of trails. Wildlife abounds on the island. Several large trees can be found on the island, including sugar maple, black walnut, and white ash. For the history of this unique place, see www.watermancenter.org/hiawatha.htm. Paddle out to Hiawatha Island to hike the trails to the observation tower. On the northeast part of the island you can find a farm house site with a creamery, privy, ice house, and cistern along with the old Hiawatha House Hotel site and a log cabin site.

Known as The Hickories because of an abundance of hickory trees, Hickories Park is a full-service campground and park operated by the Town of Owego. It offers camping facilities, picnic areas, fitness trails, playgrounds, fishing, sport fields and restrooms. Or, plan your paddle to be there on a Wednesday evening during the summer for a lawn concert.

Paddling Directions:
- From launch site #1 or #2, head left, downstream.

Morning mist rises on the Susquehanna River.

- Continue downstream after Hiawatha Island as far as you like. You'll pass The Hickories (a.k.a. Hickories Park) on the right and paddle under the bridge connecting I-86 and Route 17C.
- Turnaround whenever you wish and bear left at Hiawatha Island.
- Turn right at the end of the island.
- The dock for access to the island will be on your right.
- Explore the island, then paddle across the channel and slightly downstream to the launch point.

Date visited:

Notes:

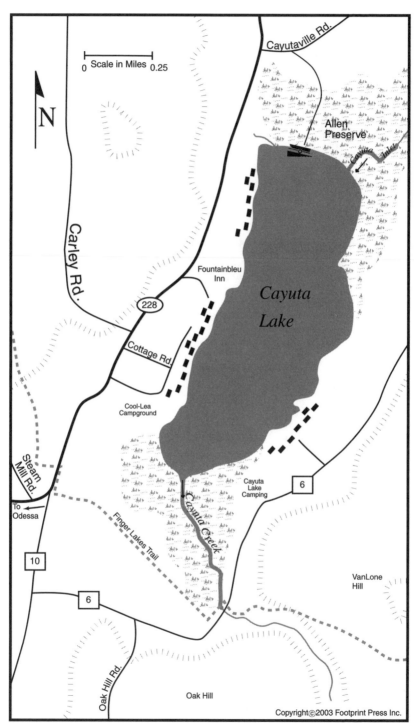

Cayuta Lake

57

CAYUTA LAKE

Location: Town of Catharine, Schuyler County

Directions: From Route 14 in Montour Falls, head east on Route 224. In Odessa, head north on Route 228. At the north end of Cayuta Lake watch for the brown DEC sign directing you to turn right onto Cayutaville Road and right again into the boat launch area.

Launch Site #1: A sloped gravel ramp near the parking area.

Best Season to Visit: Spring, summer and fall

Nearby Campgrounds: Cool-Lea Campground, on Cayuta Lake, State Route 228, Odessa, New York 14869
(607) 594-3500, www.coolleacamp.com
Cayuta Lake Camping, 2457 County Road 6, Alpine NY 14805-9756, (607) 594-2366
The Fontainbleau Inn B&B, on Cayuta Lake 2800 State Route 228, Alpine, NY 14805 (607) 594-2008

Paddling Distance: Cayuta Lake is 2 miles long

Estimated Time to Paddle: 2-3 hours

Difficulty:

Other Activities: Fish, swim

Amenities: None

Dogs: OK

Admission: Free

Contact: DEC, Region 8
276 Sing Sing Road, Suite 1, Horseheads, NY 14845
(607) 739-0809
www.dec.state.ny.us

Cayuta or Little Lake is 2 miles long and covers an area of nearly four hundred acres. It's a clear body of water with a nice mix of developed and wild shores. From the launch at the north end, you can paddle up the inlet (0.5 mile each way) or follow the eastern shore (less developed) to the south end and paddle down the outlet (Cayuta Creek) until the County Route 6 bridge (2.6 miles each way). This is where the Finger Lakes Trail crosses below Cayuta Lake.

Cayuta Inlet is home to rare freshwater sponges that are sensitive to pollutants and disturbance, but thrive in clear, clean, calcareous streams like this one. Other aquatic organisms use the sponges as homes. The area (called the James W. and Helene D. Allen Preserve) is a favorite study area of students from Cornell University.

Paddling Directions:
- Explore at will.

Date visited:

Notes:

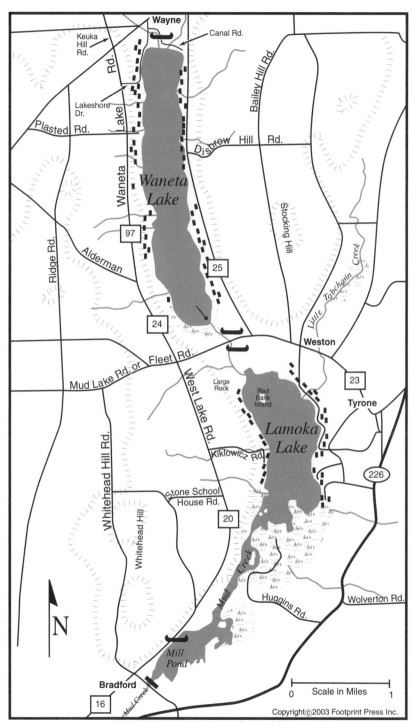

Waneta & Lamoka Lakes

58

WANETA & LAMOKA LAKES

Location: Town of Tyrone, Schuyler County

Directions: These lakes are nestled at the southeast side of Keuka Lake. From Route 226 (which runs north from Savona on Route 17 / I-86) turn west on County Route 23 in Tyrone. County Route 23 (also called Mud Lake Road or Fleet Road) runs between Waneta and Lamoka Lakes. The parking area is on both sides of County Route 23, east of the channel that connects the lakes.

Launch & Take-out Site #1: A sloped cement ramp is on one side and a sloped grass launch on the other along County Route 23 that runs between Waneta and Lamoka Lakes. There is a small dock, but it's too high for access by a kayak.

Launch & Take-out Site #2: At the southwest end of Lamoka Lake you can launch along County Route 20, just north of Bradford where the road parallels the pond.

Launch & Take-out Site #3: You can access the water in Wayne at the northern end of Waneta Lake, but it requires dragging the boat up or down a steep slope. It's along a canal found by aiming left of the church if you're paddling or by heading south on Lakeshore Drive to the corner of Canal Road if you're driving. This first bridge on the canal can't be paddled through.

Best Season to Visit: Spring, summer and fall

Paddling Distance: Total (Wayne to Bradford): 8 miles
Waneta Lake is 3 miles long
Lamoka Lake is 1.5 miles long
Mud Creek & Mill Pond (north of the dam) are 2 miles long

Estimated Time to Paddle: A few hours or spend all day

Difficulty: ▶━━━

Other Activities: Fish, swim

Amenities: Porta-potty at the parking area on Route 23

Dogs: OK

Admission: Free

The northernmost of the two lakes, Waneta sits at 1,903 feet elevation and is 3 miles long. Excavations near shore have revealed a 5,000-year-old Algonkin Indian settlement. Water flows southerly through the channel into Lamoka Lake, which sits at 1,093 feet elevation. It's 1.5-miles long, followed by 2 miles of swamp and Mill Pond to a dam at the southern end. The outflow of these lakes is called Mud Creek. It flows south into the Cohocton River.

The channel between the lakes can be paddled. You can also paddle through the culvert under County Route 23, although the clearance is low. When we paddled the channel in early June, it was afloat in yellow lilies ready to burst open and dotted with an aquatic plant covered in small white blossoms. We scared up herons, ducks and red-winged blackbirds along the way. In Lamoka Lake the carp were spawning—taking leaps in the air.

Head north to explore the marshes at the south end of Waneta Lake. Or, head south into Lamoka Lake. You can spend all day exploring all the nooks and crannies or have a short paddle around Red Bank Island (it's 0.5 mile from the north end of Lamoka Lake). Red Bank Island is private land (owned by NYSEG), but it isn't posted. The signs only say "no camping." It appears to be a heavily used island for swimming and picnics. A tree rope dangles from a branch overhanging the water inviting you to swing out. The south and east sides are sloped for easy beach landings. Since building of the dam, the island covers 3 acres. Before the dam it covered 30 acres and was home to James Pitcher, the "hermit of Red Bank." Mr. Pitcher lived in a log cabin surrounded by gardens and supplemented his living by renting boats.

Waneta Lake has more cottages and motor boat activity. Lamoka has cottages on the northeast shore and is the prettier of the two lakes. It has a nice mix of wild and developed shores. The current in and between the lakes is very minor, so you can easily paddle upstream.

Paddling Directions:
   • Explore at will.

Date visited:

Notes:

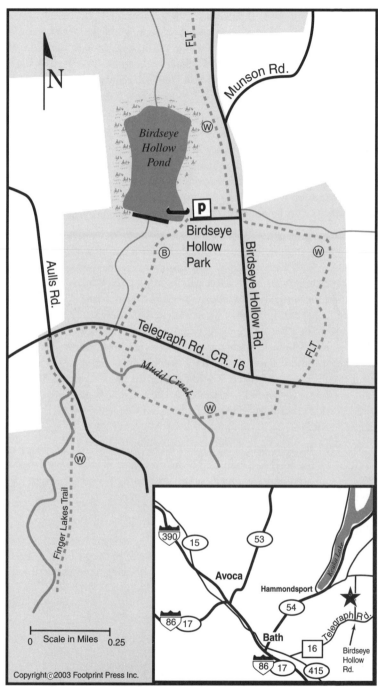

Birdseye Hollow Pond

59

BIRDSEYE HOLLOW POND

Location:	Bradford, Steuben County
Directions:	From Bath, follow Route 415 east, then County Route 16 (Telegraph Road) east. Turn left (N) onto County Road 96 (Birdseye Hollow Road). Birdseye Hollow County Park will be 0.4 mile north, on the left.

Launch & Take-out Site: From the large parking area, it's a 50-yard carry down a gravel path or across mowed grass to a grassy, sloped launch area.

Best Season to Visit: Spring, summer and fall

Paddling Distance: It's 0.5 mile around the pond

Estimated Time to Paddle: 0.5 - 1 hour

Difficulty: ▶━━━━

Other Activities:	Fish, hike, bird watch, playground (no swimming)
Amenities:	Picnic area, Porta-potty
Dogs:	OK on leash
Admission:	Free
Contact:	DEC Division of Forestry, Region 8 7291 Coon Road, Bath, NY 14810-9728 (607) 776-2165
	Steuben County Public Works - Parks 3 East Pulteney Square, Bath, NY 14810 (607) 776-9631

Birdseye Hollow Pond was formed by damming Mud Creek. It's a scenic pond, encircled by swampy areas and teeming with geese. Bring your binoculars and enjoy a day of paddling and bird watching.

The pond sits in Birdseye Hollow County Park, which itself is inside Birdseye Hollow State Forest. A boardwalk leads to an observation deck overlooking the pond. The Finger Lakes Trail winds through the forest, creating a 2-mile loop hike via blue and white blazed trails.

An observation deck extends into Birdseye Hollow Pond.

Paddling Directions:

- From the launch area, the dam and spillway are to your left. Head right toward the end of the observation deck and explore the marshy perimeter.

Date visited:

Notes:

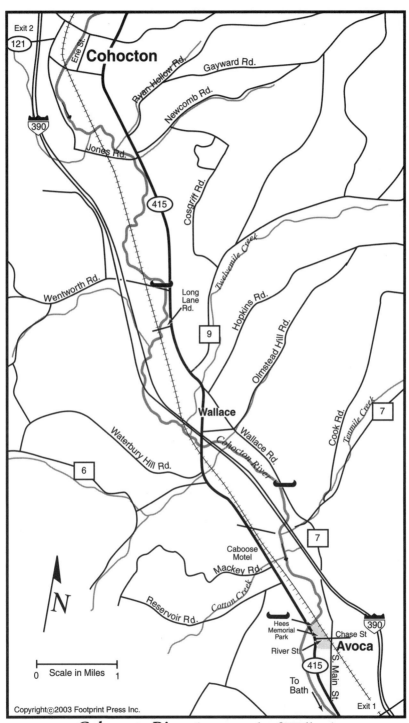

Cohocton River (start north of Wallace)

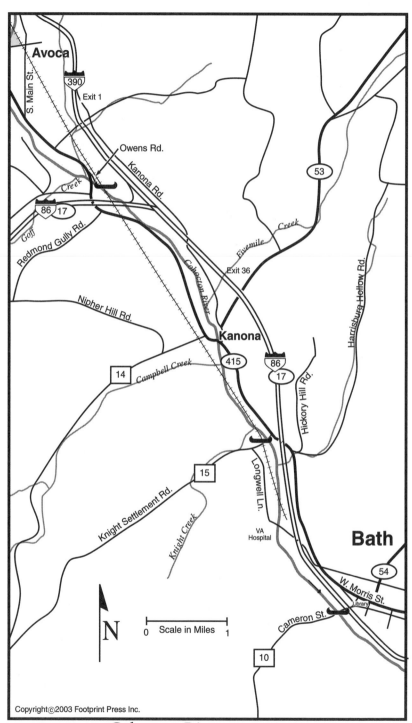

Cohocton River (end at Bath)

60

COHOCTON RIVER
(Wallace to Bath)

Location:	Wallace, Avoca, Kanona and Bath, Steuben County
Directions:	Wallace sits midway between Cohocton and Avoca. From the south take exit 1 (Avoca) off I-390 to Route 415 north. After Wallace, turn left on Wentworth Road. From the north take exit 2 (Cohocton) off I-390 and follow Route 415 south through Cohocton. Wentworth Road will be a right.
Launch Site #1:	Off Wentworth Road there is a 6-car parking lot at the river and a 50-foot carry to a grassy landing for launching.
Launch Site #2:	A parking area labeled "Cohocton River Special Trout & Fishing Area" on Wallace Road, south of Wallace.
Launch Site #3:	A gravel road between the river and Hees Memorial Park leads to a possible launch spot. Hees Memorial Park is off Route 415 at the north end of Avoca.
Launch Site #4:	A 10-car, DEC parking lot and easy launch off Owens Road (off Route 415, just north of I-86).
Launch Site #5:	A 2-car parking area on Knight Settlement Road, off Route 415, north of Bath.
Take-out Site:	The Cameron Street bridge in Bath. From Route 415 (heading south into Bath) turn right (SE) onto West Morris Street, then right (S) onto Cameron Street.

Best Season to Visit: Spring and summer (the area is hunted in fall)

Nearby Campgrounds: Tumble Hill Campground, 10551 Atlanta Back Road, Cohocton 14826, (585) 384-5248

Caboose Motel, State Route 415, Avoca 14809 (607) 566-2216

Campers Haven, Knight Settlement Road, Bath 14810 (607) 776-0328

Babcock Hollow Campground, Babcock Hollow Road, Bath 14810, (607) 776-7185

Hickory Hill Camping Resort, 7531 Mitchellsville Road, Bath 14810, (607) 776-4345

Paddling Distance: Total: 14.9 miles

Wentworth Road to Wallace Road: 3.6 miles

Wallace Road to Hees Memorial Park: 2.3 miles

Hees Memorial Park to Owens Road: 2.4 miles
Owens Road to Knight Settlement Road: 4.2 miles
Knight Settlement Rd. to Cameron Street: 2.4 miles

Estimated Time to Paddle: 3 hours in spring, 7 hours in summer

Difficulty:  (some riffles, 8-10 feet/mile gradient, climbs to 4 paddles in spring)

Water Level Information: http://waterdata.usgs.gov/ny/nwis/route (gauge 01527500 is in Avoca, gage 01528320 is in Bath)

Other Activities: Fish (this is a public trout stream)

Amenities: Hees Memorial Park has picnic tables, pavilions and Porta-potties.

Picnic tables at the Owens Road parking area.

Rental boats and shuttle service on the Canisteo, Cohocton and Tioga Rivers is available from Triple Creek Outfitters,1654 River Road, Lindley, NY 14858, (607) 523-8905

Dogs: OK

Admission: Free

Contact: DEC, Region 8
7291 Coon Road, Bath, NY 14810
(607) 776-2165

The Cohocton River winds through pasture lands.

Expect beautiful scenery of verdant farmlands, alder wetlands and forested hills with an abundance of wildlife and a clear water stream with a rocky bottom. Also expect to hear noise from nearby highways. Valleys were popular passageways for early settlers and remain so today with our superhighways. The waterway varies from 15 to 45 feet wide.

The Cohocton River starts near the Livingston - Steuben County border and flows for 60 miles to the Tioga River. It is fed by many tributaries and underground springs that give it a good year-round supply of water. It's a popular brown trout fishing stream. It's also popular fall hunting grounds as evidenced by the tree stands and hunting blinds that dot the shore.

You can begin farther upstream at Atlanta or Cohocton, but you'll find more impediments such as shallow water, downed trees and plenty of rocks. Even in the section described here, if you paddle in low water conditions, you may have to pull though some areas. In spring the flow is fast and the deep water presents ripples and a few chutes. You should find ample opportunity to take breaks along shore.

Paddling Directions:
- From the Wentworth Road launch site, head downstream.
- Pass some old bridge abutments.
- Pass under an old farm bridge at Long Lane Road, then quickly under a railroad bridge.

Paddling under a bridge on the Cohocton River.

- Pass under the huge double bridges of I-390, separated by a greater than usual distance.
- Pass under a railroad bridge, followed by the Route 415 bridge near Wallace, then quickly the two bridges of I-390 again, followed by a short drop.
- The channel splits around several islands with sharp turns and chutes.
- A parking area/launch site off Wallace Road will be on the left.
- Pass under your third set of I-390 twin bridges.
- Pass old bridge abutments.
- A downed tree blocks the creek bed where streams merge into the creek from each side. It's easy to portage around it.
- A railroad bridge followed by the Route 415 bridge will signal your arrival at Avoca. Between the two, on the left is Hees Memorial Park.
- You're now closed in by flood control banks.
- Pass several big islands (picnic time anyone?) then Goff Creek merges from the right.
- Pass under another Route 415 bridge. On the left (off Owens Road) is a DEC 10-car parking area, picnic tables and easy landing area.
- Pass under twin bridges of I-86.
- More big islands, then abutments from an old bridge in Kanona, followed quickly by a Route 415 bridge.
- Pass the small Knight Settlement Road (County Road 15) bridge. (Parking is available here for 2 cars.)
- Pass under a railroad bridge. To your right is the Bath VA Hospital.
- Pass under a bridge. You're now in the outskirts of Bath in a wide, grassy flood plain.
- Take-out is at the next bridge (Cameron Street), downstream, left.

Date visited:

Notes:

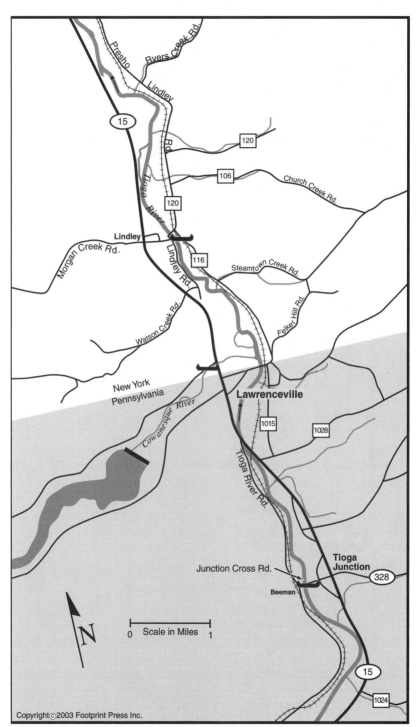

Tioga River (start at Tioga Junction, PA)

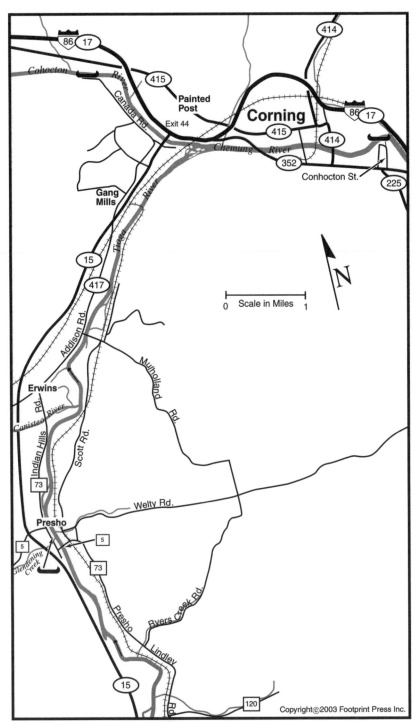

Tioga River (end at Presho, NY)

61

TIOGA RIVER
(Tioga Junction, PA to Presho, NY)

Location: Tioga Junction and Lawrenceville, PA and Lindley, and Presho, Steuben County, NY

Directions: From I-86 (old Route 17) take exit 44 to Route 15 south. The divided highway will end. Continue south over the Pennsylvania border and through Lawrenceville. In Tioga Junction turn right onto Junction Cross Road. Turn left onto a dirt lane before the bridge over Tioga River.

Launch Site #1: Southeast of the Junction Cross Road bridge is a dirt pull-off area with a short bank to rocks at shore. When parking, do not block the dry hydrant.

Alternate Launch Site: You can launch into the Cowanesque River and paddle down to the Tioga River. The launch site is at the southwest corner of the Route 15 bridge over Cowanesque River at the NY/PA border. Park in front of the Laser Car Wash on Route 15 and follow the sloped dirt roadway to below the bridge to launch at an easy gravel shore.

Launch Site #2: From Route 15 in Lindley, turn east on Morgan Creek Road at the flashing light. Turn left at the "T" then park at the dirt pull-off to the right just before the road over the bridge. Do not block the dry hydrant. A sloped grass bank leads to the water.

Take-out Site: From Route 15 turn east on County Route 5 at Presho. Turn right at the "T," then left into a large gravel parking area across from the white Presho United Methodist Church. A gradual ramp leads to a large gravel bank where Glendening Creek meets the river.

Best Season to Visit: Late spring and early summer

Nearby Campgrounds: Sunflower Acres Family Campground, 8355 Tinkertown Road, Addison, NY 14801 (607) 523-7756, sunfloweracres@aol.com

Paddling Distance: Total: 10.5 miles (Tioga Junction to Presho)
Junction Cross Road to Lindley: 5.9 miles
Route 15 (Cowanesque River) to Lindley: 3.0 miles

Lindley to Presho: 4.6 miles
Presho to Mulholland Road: 3.1 miles
Mulholland Road to Conhocton Street: 5.9 miles
(see Chemung River on page 243)

Estimated Time to Paddle: 3-4 hours in spring

Difficulty: (moving water with riffles and fast water around islands)

Water Level Information: http://waterdata.usgs.gov/pa/nwis/uv (gauge #01518700 is at Tioga Junction, PA, the start of this segment) (gage #01520000 is on the Cowanesque River near Lawrenceville, PA) http://waterdata.usgs.gov/ny/nwis/uv (gage #01526500 is on the Tioga River near Erwins) (gage #01529950 is on the Chemung River at Corning)

Other Activities: Fish, bird watch

Amenities: Rental boats and shuttle service on the Canisteo, Cohocton and Tioga Rivers is available from Triple Creek Outfitters,1654 River Road, Lindley, NY 14858, (607) 523-8905

Dogs: OK

Admission: Free

Historically the Tioga River (part of the Chemung and Susquehanna River Basin that feeds to Chesapeake Bay) flooded regularly. After the 1972 flood caused by hurricane Agnes, three large dams were built in Pennsylvania to help control the water level. The section described here begins below the dams. At Tioga Junction, the Tioga River is creek-like, as a small waterway with shallows and minor ripples. Downstream it gets wider and deeper. Above Lawrenceville it is decidedly river-like with lots of islands to paddle around.

Paddling Directions:
- From the Junction Cross Road launch, head downstream under the cement bridge.
- Pass under a rusted railroad bridge, then shortly the cement Route 15 bridge.
- Pass under the cement bridge in Lawrenceville. (There is marginal access through a weedy bank upstream, left.)
- Cowanesque River will merge from the left as outflow from the Cowanesque Dam.
- Stay to the right in the main channel to pass around a large island.
- Paddle under the arched, green metal bridge in Lindley. (Access is downstream, left).

Solo canoeing can be exhilarating on a river.

- Pass under the high, silver-railed County Route 5 bridge in Presho.
- Shortly Glendening Creek merges from the left. The take-out point is the gravel beach to the left just after the creek, before the cement abutments and power lines over the water.

   Note: If you continue downstream, you'll pass the light blue superstructure bridge of Mulholland Road in Erwins in 3.1 miles. It was under construction in 2003, so we can't comment on access near this bridge. Further downstream the Cohocton River merges from the left and the merged waterway becomes the Chemung River. The first take-out point is past 3 more bridges, at a right bend, at the end of Conhocton Street in Corning. It's 9.0 miles from Presho to the Conhocton Street access site. (See the map on page 243.)

Date visited:

Notes:

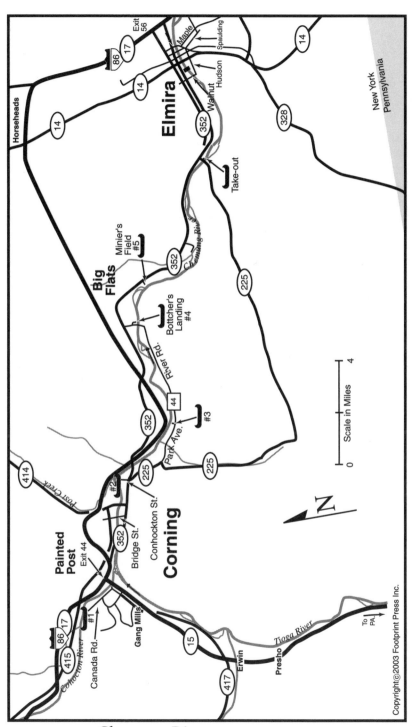

Chemung River (Corning to Elmira)

62

CHEMUNG RIVER
(Corning to Elmira)

Location: Painted Post, Corning, Big Flats and Elmira, Steuben & Chemung Counties

Directions: From I-86 (old Route 17) take exit 44 to Route 15 south. Take the first exit to Route 417, but instead of turning left onto Route 417 south, turn right onto Canada Road. Canada Road will bend left, then pass Cinderella Baseball Fields. At the end, across from Lynn Morse Drive, turn right into Kinsella Park (no sign). Drive to the end where there's a stone beach along the Cohocton River.

Launch Site #1: In Kinsella Park you can drive to the shore on a stone beach along the Cohocton River.

Launch Site #2: From Route 352 in Corning (opposite the northern terminus of Route 225), turn north onto Conhocton Street. At a bend in the road, continue straight, uphill on an unmarked, gravel drive. You can drive to and launch from a flat dirt shore.

Launch Site #3: From Route 352 in Corning, head south on Route 225. Go straight when Route 225 bends sharply, onto Park Avenue/River Road/County Route 44. Watch to the left for a brown and yellow DEC sign "Chemung River Fishing Access Site." From the DEC parking area, 17 cement steps lead into the water.

Launch Site #4: Heading east on River Road (County Route 44), it will bend north to cross over Chemung River. Immediately after the bridge (northeast side) is a colorful sign for "Bottcher's Landing." Turn right on the gravel drive at the sign. At the parking area is a sloped cement launch.

Launch Site #5: From Route 352, north of the river, watch for soccer fields (Minier's Field) and a brown and yellow DEC sign "Chemung River Fishing Access Site" on the right (if you're heading east). The paved drive leads to a parking area and mud slope.

Take-out Site: Follow Route 352 east to Route 225 south. Take a quick left at the brown and yellow DEC sign and follow the gravel drive to a parking area with a wide, sloped gravel launch.

Best Season to Visit: Summer and fall

Paddling Distance: Total: 17.0 miles

Kinsella Park to Conhocton Street: 4.1 miles (2 hrs.)
Conhocton Street to River Road: 2.7 miles (1.5 hrs.)
River Road to Bottcher's Landing: 3.6 miles (2 hrs.)
Bottcher's Landing to Route 352: 1.4 miles (1 hr.)
Route 352 to Route 225: 5.2 miles (2.5 hrs.)

Estimated Time to Paddle: 9 - 11 hours

Difficulty: (From Kinsella Park through Corning - moving water with riffles and minor white water)
(On the Chemung River - some riffles)

Water Level Information: http://waterdata.usgs.gov/ny/nwis/uv (gauge #01529500 is the Cohocton River upstream at Campbell, gauge #01529950 is the Chemung River at Corning, gage #01530332 is the Chemung River at Elmira)

Other Activities: Fish, bird watch

Amenities: Kinsella Park has a pavilion, grills, picnic tables, a small playground, a nature trail and ball fields.
Today's Tom Sawyer offers rentals and shuttles on the Chemung River from Corning to Elmira, 56 Golden Glow Drive, Elmira, NY 14905 (607) 734-3804, www.todaystomsawyer.com

Dogs: OK

Admission: Free

Contact: Chemung Basin River Trail Partnership
Southern Tier Central Regional Planning & Development Board (Jennifer Fais, co-chair)
145 Village Square, Painted Post, NY 14870
(607) 962-5092, www.stcplanning.org

Waters from the Cohocton and Tioga Rivers merge at Corning to form the Chemung River. Downstream the Chemung River joins the Susquehanna on its journey to Chesapeake Bay and the Atlantic Ocean. Early 19th century settlers used these waterways as a major transportation route. Chemung means "big horn" or "place of the horn" in the Algonquin Indian language because in 1757 they discovered a wooly mammoth tusk along the river bank that dated back to the ice ages. Where the Cohocton and Tioga Rivers meet to form the Chemung River is the town of Painted

Paddling on the Chemung River.

Post. This was a sacred place to the Iroquois Indians who placed a painted post to mark the confluence.

A 38-mile stretch of the Chemung River is now designated as the Chemung Basin River Trail. Beginning in 1999 a partnership of private and public organizations formed to build river access points and promote the riverway. It's still a work in progress. They are discussing allowing camping on the islands. The partnership coordinates an annual 6-mile Chemung River Float each spring with return shuttle service. For details call (607) 962-5092 or (607) 734-4453. They also publish a Chemung Basin River Trail Guide. To obtain one, send $2 to the Steuben County Conference and Visitors Bureau, 5 West Market Street, Corning, NY 14830.

Launching at Kinsella Park puts you in the clear, rocky-bottomed Cohocton River. Expect some ripples in the moving water. It soon merges with the Tioga River (see page 239) to become the Chemung River and flows through the developed Corning area. Road noise will be your companion through this section, but the shore is devoid of buildings due to the history of flooding (including a major flood in 1972 when water crested 25 feet above normal). Instead, you'll find willow trees and grassy slopes after shoreline rocks. Past Corning the surroundings become more rural and you'll find a gentle, lazy river with warm and usually deep water. The Chemung River seems small compared to the large valley it passes through.

Notice the cliffs between Big Flats and West Elmira (downstream from launch site #5, Minier's Field). They're home to a plant community that's unique to New York State. Overhead you may spot red-tailed hawks, ospreys, bald eagles and maybe even a golden eagle during spring or fall migration time.

Paddling Directions:
- From Kinsella Park, head downstream in the Cohocton River. It's a small, clear stream in a wide grass valley enclosed by dikes.
- Pass under the Route 15 bridge.
- The Cohocton River merges with the Tioga River in a maze of islands. Just pick a channel and continue downstream. The waterway will now be considerably wider, deeper and murkier.
- Pass under the Route 352 bridge and through the heart of Corning.
- Pass under the Bridge Street bridge with its green metal superstructure.
- Pass under a pedestrian bridge then quickly the Route 414 bridge.
- To the right, at the inside of a right bend is launch site #2 at the end of Conhocton Street. It's a flat dirt shore.
- Shortly after the Conhocton Street launch site, Post Creek merges from the left.
- I-86 (old Route 17) parallels the left shore.
- Pass under the large brown Route 352 highway bridge.
- The waterway becomes more scenic with wooded shores.
- Watch to the right for cement steps leading up a bank. This is launch site #3 to River Road.
- The river is now wide and open with periodic islands.
- Pass under the green Route 44 highway bridge. Downstream, left is the cement sloped launch of access site #4, Bottcher's Landing.
- Paddle around additional large islands. If you want to find launch site #5 (Minier's Field, Route 352), stay in the left channel around islands. There's a dirt slope at this access site on the left shore where islands separate the channel.
- High hills now close in on the valley. Watch for a resident eagle.
- Pass under the green Route 225 highway bridge. Downstream, left is the take-out point, a wide sloped gravel launch.

Note: As of 2003 the access site labeled #7 on the Chemung
Basin River Trail Guide (at the end of Grove Street in Elmira)
had not been built. Below this is a dam.

Date visited:

Notes:

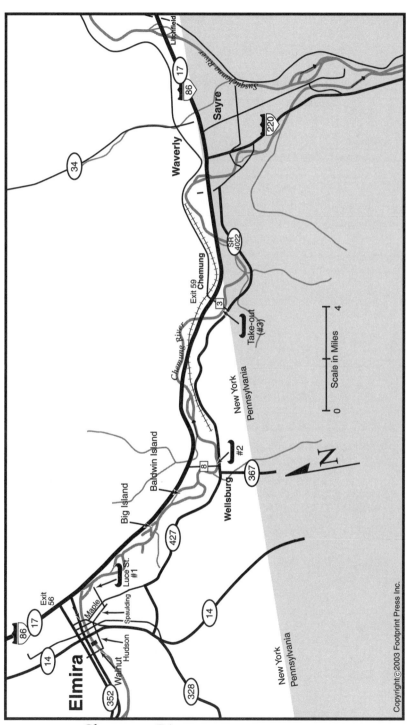

Chemung River (Elmira to the PA border)

63

CHEMUNG RIVER
(Elmira to the PA border)

Location: Elmira and Wellsburg, Chemung County

Directions: From I-86 (old Route 17) in Elmira, take exit 56 to
                     Route 352. Turn south onto Route 14 and cross the
                     Chemung River. Turn left onto Hudson Street. It will
                     bend and become Spaulding Street. Turn left onto Luce
                     Street. Follow Luce Street to the end and continue
                     straight on the gravel road past the DEC sign
                     "Chemung River Fishing Access Site."

Launch Site #1: The DEC fishing access site at the end of Luce Street
                     offers a sloped cement launch.

Launch Site #2: Take Route 427 east out of Elmira to Wellsburg. Turn
                     north on County Route 8 and cross the bridge over the
                     Chemung River. Just over the bridge, turn right at the
                     DEC sign to find a sloped cement launch.

Take-out Site (#3): Continue east on Route 427, then turn left onto
                     County Route 3 toward I-86. Cross over the bridge,
                     then turn left on an unmarked gravel road that leads to
                     shore, upstream, left of the bridge.

Best Season to Visit: Summer and fall

Paddling Distance: Total: 12.8 miles
                     Luce Street to County Route 8: 6.4 miles (3.5 hrs.)
                     County Route 8 to County Route 3: 6.4 miles (3.5 hrs.)

Estimated Time to Paddle: 6 - 8 hours hours

Difficulty: (some riffles)

Water Level Information: http://waterdata.usgs.gov/ny/nwis/uv (gauge
                     #01530332 is on the Chemung River at Elmira)

Other Activities: Fish, bird watch

Amenities: At launch site #2 (County Route 8) there's a pavilion,
                     a Porta-potty, picnic tables and grills

Dogs: OK

Admission: Free

Contact:	Chemung Basin River Trail Partnership

Southern Tier Central Regional Planning &
    Development Board (Jennifer Fais, co-chair)
145 Village Square, Painted Post, NY 14870
(607) 962-5092, www.stcplanning.org

Once you leave the busy Elmira area, you'll be in rural landscapes, although I-86 is never far from shore. See pages 245-247 for a description of the Chemung River.

Paddling Directions:
- From the DEC fishing access site at the end of Luce Street in Elmira, head downstream.
- Pass Big Island then a bigger island called Baldwin Island.
- Pass under the cement highway bridge of County Route 8. A sloped cement ramp is downstream, left.
- Paddle around more islands, then under the big I-86 bridges.
- Pass under a railroad bridge, then I-86 bridges again.
- The take-out point is upstream, left of the green County Route 3 highway bridge.

Date visited:

Notes:

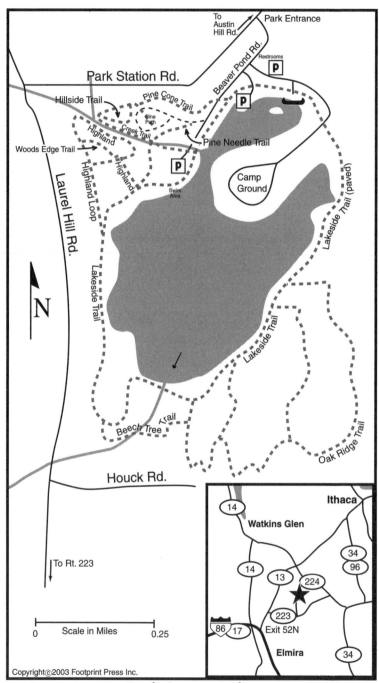

Park Station Lake

64

PARK STATION LAKE
(Beaver Pond)

Location:	Erin, Chemung County
Directions:	From Route 224 in the northeast corner of Chemung County, turn west on Route 223, then right (N) on Austin Hill Road. Watch for the entrance to Park Station Recreation Center on the left. Inside the park, take the first left and watch to the right for a small parking area along the lake.
	Caution: Do not attempt to approach from the west. Walker Hill and Burlingame are very rough roads.

Launch & Take-out Site: A sloped gravel launch at a 4-car parking area

Best Season to Visit: Spring, summer and fall

Nearby Campgrounds: A year-round campground (tent and RV) is available within this park (607-739-9164)

Paddling Distance: Approximately 2 miles around the lake

Estimated Time to Paddle: 1 - 2 hours

Difficulty: ▶──●══

Other Activities: Fish, hike, bird watch, camp, picnic, swim

Amenities: Canoe, rowboat and paddleboat rentals, restrooms

Dogs: OK on leash <8 feet long

Admission: $6 / vehicle Memorial Day to Labor Day
Paddling is allowed 7 AM - sunset, April 1 - October 31

Regulations: PFDs are required, boats on trailers require a permit

Contact: Park Station Recreation Center
2 West Beaver Pond Road, Erin, NY 14838
(607) 739-9164

Park Station Recreation Center sits on top of high hills. The centerpiece is the man-made, 100-acre lake, which is popular with paddlers, fishermen, and swimmers.

In the late 1800s Park Hill was named to honor residents Robert and Alexander Park. After a railway line was built in 1892 the community boomed and became known as Park Station. Park Station's population dwindled with the passing of the railroad and timber industries. In 1979 the creek was dammed as part of a plan to improve local soil and water resources and the area became a public recreation center. The hillsides surrounding the lake are criss-crossed with a 6.2-mile network of hiking trails.

Paddling Directions:
    • Explore at will.

Date visited:

Notes:

Definitions

Abutments: Pillars of stone and/or cement that support or used to support a bridge.

Aqueduct: A stone, wood, or cement trough built to carry canal water over an existing creek or river. The world's largest aqueduct for its time was built in Rochester to span the Genesee River. Eleven stone arches were erected, spanning 804 feet, to withstand the annual floods of this wild river.

ATV: All-terrain vehicle

Bog: An acid-rich, wet, poorly drained, spongy area characterized by plants such as sedges, heaths, and sphagnum.

Chute: A place where water gets squeezed to run quickly through a narrow passage.

Class I water: Waterways are categorized into classes from I to VI based on level of paddling difficulty. Class I is clear, wide channels with small waves, obstructions or hazards.

Class II water: A larger or narrower waterway with rapids of moderate difficulty and minimal obstructions or hazards.

CCC: Civilian Conservation Corps - a depression era work force that built public works projects across the USA. Many of the facilities in our parks (shelters, walkways, etc.) resulted from CCC projects.

Dam: A barrier constructed across a waterway to control the flow or raise the level of water.

DEC: Department of Environmental Conservation

Dike: An earthen bank constructed to hold water.

DPW: Department of Public Works

Drumlin: An elongated or oval hill created from glacial debris.

Dry hydrant: A spigot that allows fire fighters to attach hoses and quickly pump water from a stream for fire fighting.

Embankment: A man-made, high dirt wall built to contain a canal such as the Great Embankment built for the Erie Canal to cross the Irondequoit Creek valley.

Esker: A long ridge formed when rivers flowed under a glacier in an ice tunnel. Rocky material accumulated on the tunnel beds, and when the glacier melted, a ridge of rubble remained.

Feeder:	A diverted stream, brook, or other water source used to maintain water level in the canal.
Gabion:	A wire mesh basket filled with earth and stones, used in constructing dams and reinforcing shorelines.
Guard gate:	A metal gate that can be lowered to stop water flow in a canal.
Kame:	A hill formed by rivers that flowed on top of a glacier and spilled over the edge depositing soil into huge piles.
Kettle hole:	A depression pond created when a large block of ice separated from a glacier. Water running off of the glacier deposited gravel and debris all around the ice block. The block melted, leaving behind a rough circular depression.
Logjam:	Trees and branches that fall into the stream, accumulate at sharp bends and create a dam.
Neoprene:	A synthetic rubber used in weather-resistant products.
Oxbow:	Rivers and streams that wind through soft soils create oxbows, or u-shaped loops.
Pool:	A deep or still place in a stream.
Portage:	To carry or drag your boat over or around an impediment.
Marsh:	An area of soft, wet land.
Meander:	To follow a winding or twisting course. It derives from the Meander River in western Turkey that is notable for its twists and turns.
PFD:	A personal floatation device or life preserver worn to keep you afloat in case of a tip over.
Riffle:	An area of fast-moving, shallow water.
Rookery:	The nesting and breeding ground of certain birds, such as great blue herons.
Slough:	Also spelled slue. A stagnant swamp, marsh, bog, or pond, especially as part of an inlet or backwater.
Strainer:	A tree across the waterway where the main current of water passes through the tree. In effect, the water passes through the tree, but you get hung up in the branches, strained out. Because of the pressure of moving water you can be trapped underwater in a strainer and drown. Strainers are also prone to bending boats in half.
Swamp:	Wet, spongy land saturated and sometimes partially or intermittently covered with water. Or, to tip your boat over & fill it with water.

Topo map: Short for topographic map. It's a map showing elevation changes using gradient lines.

USGS: United States Geological Survey, the branch of government that produces topographic maps.

Waste weir: A dam along the edge of a canal that allows overflow water to dissipate to a side waterway. A type of spillway.

Weir: A dam placed across a river or canal to raise or divert the water, as for a millrace, or to regulate or measure the flow.

White water: Turbulent water that creates frothy white caps.

WPA: Works Progress Administration

Canoe & Kayak Rentals

Rentals in Ontario, Wayne, Yates, Seneca, Cayuga, Onondaga and Oswego Counties:

Canandaigua Sailboarding
11 Lakeshore Drive, Canandaigua, NY
(585) 394-8150

Canalside Rentals/Lakeside Rentals
locations include:
Macedon at Lock 30, Palmyra at Canal Marina, Waterloo at Oak Island
Park, Seneca Falls
(585) 377-5980, www.canalsiderentals.com

Reagan's Canoe & Kayak Livery
440 Hall Road, Himrod, NY 14842
(607) 243-9100, www.reaganscanoe.com

Rent-A-Ride
165 Water Street, Lyons, NY
(315) 946-3312

Seayaker Outfitters
4300 Canandaigua Road, Walworth, NY 14568
(315) 524-9295, www.seayaker.com

Rentals in Steuben, Schuyler, Tompkins, Chemung and Tioga Counties:

Cayuga Boat Rentals & Ferry
Cass Park off Route 89, Ithaca
(607) 277-5072

Cool-Lea Campground
Kayutah Lake, Route 228, Odessa, NY 14869
(607) 594-3500, www.coolleacamp.com

Leisure Livin' Camping & Resort / Canoe Trips
PO Box 242, River Road, Nichols, NY 13812
(877) 319-8393, www.leisurelivin.com
Rental includes free shuttle upstream on the Susquehanna River.

North Country Kayak & Canoe
665 West Lake Road, Hammondsport, NY 14840
(607) 868-7456

Puddledockers Boat Rental / Charter
704 1/2 N. Buffalo Street, Ithaca, NY 14850
(607) 273-0096, www.puddledockers.com

Reagan's Canoe & Kayak Livery
440 Hall Road, Himrod, NY 14842
(607) 243-9100, www.reaganscanoe.com

Terrapin Outfitters
219 N. Franklin Street, Watkins Glen, NY
(607) 535-5420

Terrapin Outfitters Inc.
PO Box 419, Trumansburg, NY 14886-0419
607-387-4826

Triple Creek Outfitters (on the Canisteo, Cohocton and Tioga Rivers)
1654 River Road, Lindley, NY 14858
(607) 523-8905

Today's Tom Sawyer (on the Chemung River from Corning to Elmira)
56 Golden Glow Drive, Elmira, NY 14905
(607) 734-3804, www.today'stomsawyer.com

Water & Wilderness (on the Susquehanna River)
6530 Route 434, PO Box 100, State Route 434, Apalachin, NY 13732
(607) 625-9922, www.waterandwilderness.com

On-site Boat Rentals Available

Guided Paddling Tours

Belfast Canoe Rental
PO Box 186, Belfast, NY 14711
(716) 365-8129

Climb Aboard the Susquehanna River Shuttle
Waterman Conservation Center
(607) 625-2221

Hemlock Canoe Works
5407 State Route 15A, PO Box 68, Hemlock, NY 14466
(585) 367-3040
www.hemlockcanoe.com

Leisure Livin' Camping & Resort / Canoe Trips
PO Box 242, River Road, Nichols, NY 13812
(877) 319-8393
www.leisurelivin.com

Pack, Paddle, Ski, Corp.
PO Box 82, South Lima, NY 14558-0082
(585) 346-5597
www.PackPaddleSki.com
Local and world-wide lessons and tours.

Paths, Peaks and Paddles Inc.
7000 S. Transit Rd., Lockport, New York 14094
(716) 625-4493
www.pathspeakspaddles.net

Puddledockers Boat Rental / Charter
704 1/2 N. Buffalo Street, Ithaca, NY 14850
(607) 273-0096
www.puddledockers.com

Rent-A-Ride
165 Water Street, Lyons, NY
(315) 946-3312

Reagan's Canoe & Kayak Livery
440 Hall Road, Himrod, NY 14842
(607) 243-9100, www.reaganscanoe.com

Seayaker Outfitters
4300 Canandaigua Road, Walworth, NY 14568
(315) 524-9295
www.seayaker.com

Sea Kayak Rochester
606 Madison Street, East Rochester, NY 14445
(585) 381-2104
www.seakayakrochester.com

Terrapin Outfitters Inc.
PO Box 419, Trumansburg NY 14886-0419
(607)387-4826

Today's Tom Sawyer (on the Chemung River from Corning to Elmira)
56 Golden Glow Drive, Elmira, NY 14905
(607) 734-3804
www.today'stomsawyer.com

Water & Wilderness
6530 Route 434, PO Box 100, State Route 434, Apalachin, NY 13732
(607) 625-9922
www.waterandwilderness.com

Shuttles and/or Liveries:

BayCreek Paddling Center (on Irondequoit Creek)
1099 Empire Blvd., Rochester, NY 14609
(585)288-2830
www.baycreek.com

Oak Orhcard Canoe & Kayak Experts (on Irondequoit Creek)
1300 Empire Blvd., Rochester, NY
(585) 288-5550
www.oakorchardcanoe.com

Paths Peaks and Paddles Inc.
7000 S. Transit Rd., Lockport, New York 14094
(716) 625-4493
www.pathspeakspaddles.net

Reagan's Canoe & Kayak Livery
440 Hall Road, Himrod, NY 14842
(607) 243-9100
www.reaganscanoe.com

Today's Tom Sawyer (on the Chemung River from Corning to Elmira)
56 Golden Glow Drive, Elmira, NY 14905
(607) 734-3804
www.today'stomsawyer.com

Triple Creek Outfitters (on the Canisteo, Cohocton and Tioga Rivers)
1654 River Road, Lindley, NY 14858
(607) 523-8905

Water & Wilderness (on the Susquehanna River)
6530 Route 434, Apalachin, NY 13732
(607) 626-9922
www.waterandwilderness.com

Paddling Clubs:

Southern Tier:
Ahwaga Canoe Club
2890 Hullsville Road, Owego, NY 13827
(607) 687-2989
www.ahwagacanoe.com

Adirondack Mountain Club - Susquehanna Chapter
www.adk.org/html/adk_susquehanna_chapter.htm

Syracuse area:
Central New York Kayak Club
www.cnykayakclub.com

Ka-Na-Wa-Ke Canoe Club
meets at Huntington Elementary School Cafeteria, Syracuse
www.tier.net/kanawake/

Adirondack Mountain Club - Onondaga Chapter
www.adk.org/html/adk_onondaga_chapter.html

Finger Lakes region:
Adirondack Mountain Club - Finger Lakes Chapter
http://people.clarityconnect.com/webpages/schwartz/adk/

General:
New York Marathon Canoe Racing
PO Box 245, Gilbertsville, NY 13776
www.nymcra.org

Canoe/Kayak Storage Systems:

Talic Sport Hammocks
316 North Goodman Street, Rochester, NY 14607
(800) 843-3307, info@talic.com
www.talic.com

Paddling Instruction:

Genesee Waterways Center
141 Elmwood Ave., Rochester, NY
(585) 328-3960
www.geneseewaterways.org

Pack, Paddle, Ski, Corp.
PO Box 82, South Lima, NY 14558-0082
(585) 346-5597, info@PackPaddleSki.com
www.PackPaddleSki.com
Local and world-wide lessons and tours.

Puddledockers Boat Rental / Charter
704 1/2 N. Buffalo Street, Ithaca, NY 14850
(607) 273-0096
www.puddledockers.com

Seayaker Outfitters
4300 Canandaigua Road, Walworth, NY 14568
(315) 524-9295
www.seayaker.com

Flow Gages

National Weather Service Northeast River Forecast center
http://www.erh.noaa.gov/er/nerfc/

- -Canandaigua Outlet
- -Oswego River
- -Fall Creek
- -Susquehanna River
- -Tioughnioga River
- -Chenango River
- -Cohocton River

- -Chemung River
- -Seneca River
- -Owasco Lake Outlet
- -Unadilla River
- -Otselic River
- -Tioga River

U.S. Geology Survey - Real Time Data for New York
http://waterdata.usgs.gov/ny/nwis/rt

Waterways by Level of Difficulty

1 Paddle:

1 Paddle:

2 Paddles:

3 Paddles:

3 Paddles:

4 Paddles:

Waterways by Length

1 to 2 Mile Paddles

3 to 5 Mile Paddles

3 to 5 Mile Paddles

6 to 10 Mile Paddles

Over 10 Mile Paddles

Waterways by Season

Paddle Spring, Summer or Fall

Paddle Spring, Summer or Fall

Paddle Spring

Paddle Summer

Paddle Spring and Summer

Paddle Spring and Summer

Paddle Summer and Fall

Paddle Fall

On-site Camping Available

Round Trip Paddling Possible

Round Trip Paddling Possible

Commercial Shuttles Available

Word Index

Word Index

Word Index

Word Index

Word Index

About the Authors

The authors, Rich and Sue Freeman, decided to make their living from what they love—being outdoors. In 1996 they left corporate jobs to spend six months hiking 2,200 miles on the Appalachian Trail from Georgia to Maine. That adventure deepened their love of the outdoors and inspired them to share this love by introducing others to the joys of hiking.

Since most people don't have the option (let alone the desire) to undertake a six-month trek, they decided to focus on short hikes, near home. The result was the first edition of *Take A Hike! Family Walks in the Rochester Area*. They went on to explore hiking, bicycling, skiing, and snowshoeing trails, waterfalls and now waterways for paddling throughout Central and Western New York State. This is their 10th guidebook.

Rich and Sue are active members of several area outdoors groups. In addition, their passion for adventure continues. They have hiked the 500-mile-long Bruce Trail in Ontario, Canada, hiked on the Florida Trail, hiked across northern Spain on the Camino de Santiago Trail and hiked a 500-mile section of the International Appalachian Trail in Quebec, Canada. They have trekked to the top of Mt. Kilimanjaro, the highest mountain in Africa. Recently (in addition to kayaking hundreds of miles of New York's waterways), they hiked the tropical forests and volcanic peaks of wild Hawaii.

On bicycles they have crossed New York State on the Erie Canalway Trail and pedaled the C&O Canal Trail from Washington D.C. to Cumberland, Maryland.

The Freemans' regularly present slide shows about their adventures. For the current schedule see www.footprintpress.com under Event Schedule. To book a slide show for your group, call (585) 421-9383. They also publish a free, monthly electronic newsletter on outdoor recreation in Central and Western New York State. For a free subscription, enter your email address on the home page at www.footprintpress.com.

Since beginning their new career writing and publishing guidebooks, the Freemans' have pared down their living expenses and are enjoying a simpler lifestyle. They now have control of their own destiny and the freedom to head into the woods and waterways for a refreshing respite when the urge strikes. Still, their life is infinitely more cluttered than when they carried all their worldly needs on their backs for six months on the Appalachian Trail.

Other Books Available from Footprint Press

Paddling

Take A Paddle - Western New York Quiet Water for Canoes & Kayaks
ISBN# 1-930480-23.7   U.S. $18.95
20 ponds and lakes plus over 250 miles of flat-water creeks
and rivers in western New York for fun on the water.

Cross-country Skiing and Snowshoeing:

Snow Trails – Cross-country Ski and Snowshoe
in Central and Western New York
ISBN# 0-9656974-52   U.S. $16.95
80 mapped locations for winter fun on skis or snowshoes.

Hiking:

Peak Experiences – Hiking the Highest Summits in NY,
County by County
ISBN# 0-9656974-01   U.S. $16.95
A guide to the highest point in each county of New York
State.

New York State County Summit Club Patch
ISBN# None   U.S. $2.00
A colorful embroidered patch to commemorate your
Peak Experiences.

Take A Hike! Family Walks in the Rochester Area
ISBN# 0-9656974-79   U.S. $16.95
60 day hikes within a 15-mile radius of Rochester, N.Y.

Take A Hike! Family Walks in the Finger Lakes & Genesee Valley Region
ISBN# 0-9656974-95   U.S. $16.95
51 day hike trails throughout central and western New York.

Bruce Trail – An Adventure Along the Niagara Escarpment
ISBN# 0-9656974-36   U.S. $16.95
Learn the secrets of long-distance backpackers on a five-week
hike in Ontario, Canada, as they explore the abandoned
Welland Canal routes, caves, ancient cedar forests, and white
cobblestone beaches along Georgian Bay.

Backpacking Trails of Central & Western New York State
ISBN# none   U.S. $2.00
A 10-page booklet describing the backpackable trails of
central and western NYS with contact information to obtain
maps and trail guides.

Other Books Available from Footprint Press

Bird Watching:

Birding in Central & Western New York – Best Trails &
Water Routes for Finding Birds
    ISBN# 1-930480-00-8   U.S. $16.95
    70 of the best places to spot birds on foot, from a car,
    or from a canoe.

Bicycling:

Take Your Bike! Family Rides in the Rochester Area
    ISBN# 1-930480-02-4   U.S. $18.95
    Converted railroad beds, paved bike paths and woods trails
    combine to create the 42 safe bicycle adventures within an
    easy drive of Rochester, N.Y.

Take Your Bike! Family Rides in the Finger Lakes &
Genesee Valley Region
    ISBN# 0-9656974-44   U.S. $16.95
    Converted railroad beds, woods trails, and little-used country
    roads combine to create the 40 safe bicycle adventures
    through central and western New York State.

Waterfall Fun:

200 Waterfalls in Central and Western New York – A Finders' Guide
    ISBN# 1-930480-00-8   U.S. $18.95
    Explore the many diverse waterfalls that dot the creeks and
    gorges of central and western New York State.

Self-help:

Alter – A Simple Path to Emotional Wellness
    ISBN# 0-9656974-87   U.S. $16.95
    A self-help manual that assists in recognizing and changing
    emotional blocks and limiting belief systems, using easy-to-
    learn techniques of biofeedback to retrieve subliminal
    information and achieve personal transformation.

For sample maps and chapters explore:
www.footprintpress.com

Yes, I'd like to order Footprint Press books:

\#

_____	_Take A Paddle - Western NY_	$18.95
_____	_Take A Paddle - Finger Lakes NY_	$18.95
_____	_200 Waterfalls in Central & Western NY_	$18.95
_____	_Peak Experiences—Hiking the Highest Summits of NY_	$16.95
_____	_NYS County Summit Club Patch_	$ 2.00
_____	_Snow Trails—Cross-country Ski & Snowshoe_	$16.95
_____	_Birding in Central & Western NY_	$16.95
_____	_Take A Hike! Family Walks in the Rochester Area_	$16.95
_____	_Take A Hike! Family Walks in the Finger Lakes_	$16.95
_____	_Take Your Bike! Family Rides in the Rochester Area_	$18.95
_____	_Take Your Bike! Family Rides in the Finger Lakes_	$16.95
_____	_Bruce Trail—Adventure Along the Niagara Escarpment_	$16.95
_____	_Backpacking Trails of Central & Western NYS_	$ 2.00
_____	_Alter—A Simple Path to Emotional Wellness_	$16.95

Sub-total $_____

NYS and Canadian residents add 8% tax $_____

Shipping is FREE

Total enclosed: $_____

Your Name: _____

Address: _____

City: _____ State (Province): _____

Zip (Postal Code): _____ Country: _____

Make check payable and mail to:
Footprint Press, Inc.
P.O. Box 645, Fishers, N.Y. 14453

Or, order through www.footprintpress.com

Footprint Press books are available at special discounts
when purchased in bulk for sales promotions,
premiums, or fund raising. Call (585) 421-9383.